DISCOVER
Your Child's

DO
FACTOR

THE DISCIPLINE QUOTIENT SYSTEM

DR. GREG CYNAUMON

DISCOVER
Your Child's

DQ

FACTOR

THE DISCIPLINE QUOTIENT SYSTEM

INTEGRITY®
PUBLISHERS
Nashville

To my wife, Jan, who is without question, the most beautiful and amazing person I've encountered in my life—
not to mention a far better parent than I will ever be.

CONTENTS

ACKNOWLEDGMENTS

Sometimes the joy of writing is compromised through the sacrifice of time with one's family and friends. Only through the grace of God and loved ones does the writing experience truly become joyful. That is why I wish to personally acknowledge the following people:

My exceptionally well-behaved children (living testimonials that the DQ Factor works)—Tracy (age eighteen) and Matthew (age seventeen). I thank you for being the wonderful young people you are. I can't imagine how I ever enjoyed life before I met you.

My parents, Myrna and Ed, and my brother and partner, Dana, and his wife, Pam—let me simply say thank you for your support.

Chip MacGregor, my agent and confidant at Alive Communications—thanks for your vision and hard work.

The Integrity team, including Byron Williamson, Joey Paul, Rob Birkhead, Kris Bearss, and Derek Bell, who constantly impress and amaze me with your vision. And to Stephanie Terry, whose writing and editing insights were matched by her ability to understand my humor, thanks! Each of you has been a blessing from God.

The 147 families comprising some 284 individuals who participated in one of the largest psychological family studies in recent years. Without you, this book would not have happened.

And finally, special thanks to each and every psychological assistant and intern who laboriously gathered and pored over thousands of transcribed pages and hundreds of audio- and videotapes so that this project would have true scientific validity.

INTRODUCTION

When it comes to self-help parenting books, my opinion has been (and continues to be) that most are not worth their weight in fruit snacks.

To put it mildly, I don't have many positive things to say about the psycho-babble found in the vast majority of parenting books that line the bookstore shelves. It's probably fair to admit that I don't tend to have much respect for the pointy-headed shrinks (my colleagues) who write them. I hesitate to paint with such a broad brush, and I pray this does not sound grandiose, but as an ex-cop turned therapist and radio talk show host, I think I am in an unusual position to judge. Over the years of conducting a daily, four-hour talk show in Los Angeles, I have read (more accurately, snoozed through) well over two hundred parenting books. Although the vast majority of the authors I've inter-viewed are very nice and well intentioned, I can count on one hand the number of truly significant literary contributions. No disrespect intended, but most parenting books should carry a label: *Made from 100 percent recycled material.* Not for the pulp content, but for the message.

Just so you know that I am being fair in my assessment, please note that I've contributed more than my share to the perpetual flow of "psychodrivel" myself. With four parenting books to my credit, only my pride prevents me from saying they were not much better than all the others. Although three of the four were favorably reviewed and reached significant sales figures, I can't really look back and say that I truly offered anything even remotely close to *life changing*. I'm certain that is the case with my first parenting book (*How to Avoid Alienating Your Kids in 10 Easy Steps*) that likely sold a grand total of twenty copies. Of course, that doesn't count the twelve books my mom purchased (I gave her a 5 percent discount, naturally) to give to her friends.

I digress; so let me get back to the issue of parenting books and my informal study as to who really purchases them. Granted, this was an unscientific study, but I firmly believe the outcome to be an accurate snapshot of how desperately we parents try to do the right thing by, and for, our kids.

Here are the results of my book-buying study:

- Moms purchase 82 percent of all parenting books, but only about 25 percent of them finish the book.

- Anecdotally (but only partially tongue-in-cheek), I believe the rest of the parenting books are purchased by men. What we don't say is that we are buying them for our wives for the specific purpose of getting our wives to fix the kids.

- I estimate that about 4 percent of dads purchase parenting books even though they subconsciously know they will never read them. They are what I term *prop books*. Just buying these books and having them sitting around makes us look and feel more highly evolved and sensitive. (Notice the reduction in forehead slope so as to diminish the resemblance to early man.)

- And finally, I do recognize that there are dads who actually purchase and *read* parenting books. The only caveat is that these are the same twelve guys who go linen shopping with their wives and listen to Yanni albums.

I have theorized, however, that the best way to validate my book-purchasing theory would be to search the bathrooms of every home—otherwise known as the library and last bastion of privacy for the American dad. Do me a favor: If you find a parenting book next to the sports page, *TV Guide*, and empty toilet paper dispenser, take a picture and nominate that guy for Dad of the Year.

All book-buying sarcasm aside, there is one particular point I need to impress on you. That point is that both parents need to understand and apply the discipline techniques you will learn in this book. To have one parent fully on board while the other enables or makes excuses for the child's misbehavior is a recipe for failure.

Therefore, as I make the broad assumption that you and your spouse are *not* sitting on the sofa reading this book simultaneously, I strongly recommend one of two things. The first would make my publisher very happy, and that would be to buy another DQ book for your spouse. While you are at it, you may want to make them delirious and buy DQ books for your entire block, but let's not go overboard. The more practical approach would be to make this book a shared activity between you and your spouse. I highly recommend that one spouse reads one chapter and, using a unique color highlighter, highlights points that he or she wants to call to the other parent's attention. Feel free to make side notes concerning your thoughts and observations about your child as well. Then, give the book to your spouse to read the same chapter. Using a different color highlighter, he or she will highlight areas in that one chapter that were especially poignant from his or her perspective. Then, the book comes back to you for your consideration of your spouse's highlighted areas. Whereas this technique takes more time to complete the book, I'm certain I am stating the obvious when I say that the results will be far more positive.

Grandiose as it may sound, I hope that you will approach this book from the perspective that it is *not just another parenting book*. Learning the four motivating reasons (DQ Factors) that cause your child or teenager to misbehave and then knowing how to fix them is a life-changing experience. You will gain the most from this experience if you enter this process without judgment and with your eyes wide open. You will learn new things and be exposed to innovative techniques. Experience has taught me that you need to approach this without preconceived ideas or conclusions. Just take it all in and learn what there is to learn first, and then form your own conclusions. Secondly, ditch any investment you may have in trying to be the perfect parent. It serves absolutely no purpose to discount what you are reading as not applying to you. It is even more damaging to read and defer the blame for your child's misbehaviors to your spouse.

The bottom line as you embark on this tour of the DQ Zoo is that it is not about judging or rating your skills and parenting acumen. Likewise, this book is not about judging your child. This book is about discovering your child's DQ Factor and then equipping you with the proper tools to work with it. You may learn that your teenager's DQ Factor #1—Bear score was the single-highest recorded score since Genghis Khan's parents evaluated him on his way out the door to conquer Asia. And you think you have problems!

What I am saying is that DQ Factor scores are fine for evaluating and adjusting disciplinary methods, but they mean nothing in the grand scale of life. They don't reflect on who you are as a person or parent any more than they reflect on who your child is as a human being. Keep it all in proper per-spective and this will be a far richer experience for you.

This book and the included breakthrough DQ Factor tests are not intended to be IQ or personality tests. Many of the tests that we therapists use are valuable in their own respect, but the truth is, you can do little to change and influence your IQ or your personality type. The DQ Factor is based on years of research that produced the existence of four predominant motivators for why children misbehave, act out, disrespect, disregard, discount, and basically thumb their little noses at us. After you have identified your child's motivation for misbehaving, you'll discover innovative and specific types of discipline and boundary tactics that have been statistically proven to be winners.

As you embark on this fascinating, entertaining, and hopefully life-changing discovery of your child's DQ Factor, please know that I believe your child is as special as you do. I also know that no one, *especially not this shrink*, knows your child as well as you do. Therefore, please regard this landmark study and subsequent advice as a formidable tool in your hands. A tool that, coupled with your instincts and common sense, will empower you to become a more effective and less stressed parent.

NEVER ACCEPT ADVICE FROM A LUNATIC

As it applies to the topic of open-mindedness, my pastor used to have a saying: Some people are so open-minded that they are in danger of their brains falling out. This applies to all forms of advice—especially advice as important as how you parent your children. If you're like me, you want to know something about the adviser before you accept all he's saying as the truth. I mean, what if I'm a card-carrying lunatic who sits on hillsides baying at the full moon? Wouldn't you want to know that before you bought into my personal and scientific theories about spanking versus bribing your kids to behave? I would.

To the best of my knowledge (note disclaimer), I am not, nor have I ever been, a lunatic. My first and only wife of twenty-two years would tell you that although I may stare at the moon on occasion, I rarely bark. As a clean-cut Christian therapist and ex-cop, you can surmise that I've never smoked pot, dropped acid, snorted cocaine, or shot heroin. The strongest drug I use is aspirin, and two of them give me a stomachache.

I should also assure you that I do not own a Ouija board, magic crystals, Tarot cards, or tea leaves. I've never been to a psychic, numerologist, mystic, fortuneteller, exorcist, or spiritual medium. In fact, I'm not even too keen on chiropractors—not because they're bad folks at all, but only because I avoid pain whenever possible. I don't read my horoscope, and I've never had an out-of-body experience or been accused of harboring demons.

You need to know that for the past eleven years, I have regularly attended and have been on pastoral staff of a mainstream evangelical, Bible-teaching church. For years I've taught adult Sunday school and been a featured lecturer at churches throughout the country. It is my practice to look at all scientific and psychological theory through a prism of my Christianity and what the Bible says about the subject. This was never more pointed than with my last book, *God Still Speaks through Dreams*. This was a prime example of a difficult topic (dream interpretation) that I examined from a biblical perspective first, and a scientific perspective second. More information about that book, other resources, and my web site are listed at the end of this book.

I mentioned above that I am an ex-police officer/detective. Perhaps you are wondering, how does a vice and narcotics detective with two kids evolve into a therapist? It was during my fifth year (of a total of ten years) in law enforcement that I came to the realization that I simply couldn't envision myself doing twenty-five more years of graveyard shifts, jelly donuts, missing my kids (not in that order), and the stress of working vice and narcotics in the Los Angeles area. It was then that I returned to college to study psychology. Upon receiving a master's degree, I left the department and ventured into private practice with Minirth-Meier Clinics—the national, evangelically based mental health clinics. Before leaving law enforcement, however, I took more than my share of ribbing from my fellow officers. Some of their favorite barbs featured remarkable phrases such as: *detective doctor, Officer Brain-shrinker,* and *Sergeant Siggie* (as in Sigmund Freud).

I found that my background as a vice and narcotics detective, SWAT team hostage negotiator, and patrol sergeant provided me with a varied perspective that my colleagues didn't have the luxury of having. This was particularly beneficial as I began to understand more about effective parenting, boundaries, and multiple forms of both effective and ineffective discipline. I continue to believe that one can learn more about human nature in one year on the streets as a cop than in five years as a psychologist.

My Own Discipline Foibles

Let me fast-forward a few years to a time when my own children reached the age where parenting skills began to be put to the test. I had transitioned out of law enforcement and was enjoying a nice private practice during the mornings and middays while also hosting a weekday, drive-time talk-radio program.

My real education all started at about the same time as I finally understood what all these parents had been complaining about over the years. Raising kids is hard work! That's also about the time I went from superhero *Doctor Dad* to *Doctor Dud.*

First, in my role as Doctor Dad, I had it all figured out. Before they got older and began to individuate (separate, develop DQ Factors as well as their own personalities), I had the sweetest, most well-behaved kids on the planet. My five-year-old daughter, Tracy (a.k.a. The Princess), was every dad's dream. She was adorable, compliant, attentive, and just seemed to exist to constantly nominate me for Dad of the Year. I theorized that my megafather status must have been a by-product of the three parenting books I'd written. Certainly my daughter was a living, breathing testimony that psychologists could indeed (gulp) raise well-behaved kids.

Sunday mornings were a celebration of what wonderful parents her mother and I were. Following the dismissal of her children's church, anyone who came within a thirteen-block perimeter of Tracy would lavish my wife and me with praise. We'd overhear Sunday school teachers commenting, "Oh, I had Tracy in my class today. Isn't Dr. Cynaumon doing a wonderful job? My goodness, if only all of our kids could have Dr. Cynaumon for a father, I'm sure they would all grow up and solve world hunger and put conservatives back into government." (Actually, the last part is my own fantasy.)

Perhaps I went a little over the top with the whole Sunday school false-idol thing, but nonetheless, my daughter was a joy to parent—back then! Even disciplining her was a day at Disneyland. On the rare occasion when she would do something wrong (completely by accident, you understand, and probably influenced by her mother), all it would take from either of us was a slight lowering of the head followed by an ever-so-subtle horizontal nod. She would freeze whatever it was she was doing, apologize, genuflect, wax my SUV, and ask for forgiveness. (Actually, the wax-my-SUV part is also a fantasy.)

My secret theory was that the other 152.5 million parents on the planet were snivelers and whiners. How tough could this parenting thing be if all it takes is a stern look and every kid within eyesight stops whatever dastardly deed he's doing, drops, and gives me fifty pushups? My goodness, I was going to bottle this look and sell it to unfortunate parents. I'd be rich!

How naive.

That's when God decided He was going to toy with me. I clearly fell from parenting grace through the birth and early development years of our second child. Many have known him by his various monikers such as Lucifer, Beelzebub, and the Great Deceiver. In our household, he simply answered to the name Matt.

Isn't it ironic? We named our precious little bundle of joy Matthew. *Matthew!*

The angels sang when he was born. Actually, I think it was my wife's hollering that set off car alarms for miles, but we named him after St. Matthew the disciple anyway. Four years later, I mostly referred to him as "your child" to my wife. Our little gift to mankind had turned four, and I theorized that our nasty little ill-tempered fire starter must have contracted a demon somewhere along the way. Looking back, my hunch is that it was probably at his third birthday party when that uninvited, six-year-old juve, dog-shaving Philistine neighbor kid crashed the party unannounced—and giftless, I might add. I never liked that kid so, if it's all the same to you, let's stipulate that he's the reason my son became a preadolescent delinquent.

Oh, and how things changed. Suddenly, volunteers disappeared from the church nursery. People started to look at my wife and me differently. Instead of loving smiles as we strode through the quad at church, people grabbed their youngsters and scurried away whispering hurtful things such as, "Don't make eye contact with the doctor." Or, "I wonder what kind of a doctor he really is?" Or the simple, yet effective, "Quack!"

Okay, perhaps I'm guilty of exaggerating here—except for the part about the neighbor kid who snuck the demon into my son's party—but my point remains: You can't rely on the parenting skills you developed with one child and expect them to fit the other. This is especially true when it comes to discipline. Whereas my daughter would respond instantly to the subtle look or disapproving nods, my son would shoot back the same look as if to say, "Hey, rookie! You don't really think that stuff is going to play here, do you?"

In the span of a few short months, Matthew had dismantled all that I had come to believe about the fine art of discipline. *Spankings?* He would receive a little swat on his behind and just stand there as if to ask, "Is that all you got, big man?" And *time-outs?* HA! TO THIS I LAUGH! Time-outs were just opportunities for him to hone his parent-torturing skills in the privacy of his room. His response to my telling him to go to his room for a fifteen-minute time-out was, "Fifteen minutes? I can't even get started in fifteen minutes. Let's make it an even thirty. And while we're at it, how about sending in the cat and the hedge trimmer . . . it's mohawk time."

It was time to break out the heavy artillery. Where were the Dobson books? He wasn't just a strong-willed child; he was the *poster boy* for strong-willed children in the free world (and possibly much of Communist Asia). I'm not sure, but I think he kept mountains of fan mail from other nasty little ill-tempered kids from all over the world under his bed.

Slowly but surely, through concerted and consistent efforts, my wife and I were able to weather the tough years. We reveled in our victory that we made it through without having to resort to tranquilizer darts or heavy medication—with him, that is. We, on the other hand, purchased stock in Excedrin.

I embarrass my son now, partly as payback because it is only fair, but more to reveal our parenting exploits to illustrate two points. The first is that, between my long career as a cop, a psychologist, and my experience with my own kids—I know exactly what parents of strong-willed children are going through. And second, parents must understand that each child (and even his DQ Factor) will evolve over a period of time. The right combination of discipline and boundaries must evolve with him as well. Again, what works with one child at age two may not work at all by the time he is four. It's like he figured out the rules and then changed them on you while you were sleeping. Likewise, the disciplinary efforts that worked with the first child likely will blow up in your face with number two. My hunch is that it is a union thing. They all got together and decided that making this easy would not do at all. Keeping us parents dangling at the end of our collective ropes gives kids power. We will discuss my parenting foibles throughout this book, but for now, I should tell you how my kids have responded to the great DQ Factor theory—in practice.

They are not yet fully grown and out on their own, but it's important to note that neither am I writing this book while they are on death row. They are no longer four and three years old respectively. My daughter is eighteen and my son is seventeen. They both have strong Christian values and beliefs, attend church regularly, are active student leaders, play sports, and have never even tried drugs or alcohol. As an ex-vice and narcotics detective, I believe I'd know. In short, my wife and I could not be more proud of them. Oh, and lest the Humane Society get a copy of this book, no cats received mohawks during my son's formative years. Crew cuts with number three clippers on the sides, perhaps, but no mohawks.

CHAPTER 1
IQ! EQ! DQ!

Let me set the tone for our venture into the parenting realm of DQ Factors. DQ stands for *Discipline Quotient* (although my wife refers to it as "Dairy Queen"). Most of us are familiar with the term IQ (*Intelligence Quotient*) and its accompanying battery of tests designed to measure intelligence. Although I am not a big fan of IQ testing and believe it falls well short of providing clinicians an accurate measure of human potential, these and similar tests have been around since the late 1800s and are widely accepted.

More recently (as of the late 1980s), EQ or *Emotional Quotient* tests have gained popularity among clinicians, teachers, and sociologists. For two decades their results have provided measurable insights into how differently each of us deals with situations.

Neither measurement, however, has been the least bit helpful to parents in their day-to-day struggle to set healthy limits and apply the right discipline for their children. Likewise, none of these tests have helped to identify why kids misbehave in the first place, let alone recommend what types of discipline and limits will work and which definitely will not.

The theory that launched my clinical (and personal) interest and study into DQ Factors had its genesis in the understanding that, although misbehaving motives appear in four specific categories, all kids misbehave for one primary goal—to feel *significant*. Therefore, to really understand the birth of DQ Factors, we have to begin with an understanding of the human search to be significant.

Both as a Christian and as a scientist, I believe that God created each of us with a clearly defined sense of *right* and *wrong*. To do right produces a sense of significance, importance, goodness, acceptance by God, parents, others—and love. To do wrong (misbehave) brings about a sense of inadequacy, disconnectedness, badness, and guilt. This point provides the DQ theory: *Misbehaving is just a symptom that your child is feeling insignificant, unimportant, and perhaps unloved.* It is your task (aided by this book) to determine why and correct it.

If you are still struggling with this concept, think of it in terms of going to the doctor with a fractured arm. The symptoms of your injury are pain, swelling, and fever. If the doctor couldn't look past your symptoms for the root cause of your discomfort, he would treat you with pain pills, anti-inflammatory meds, and aspirin. Eventually your arm might heal well enough by itself, but it is likely going to cause ongoing problems. The analogy equates to this: When your child misbehaves, you have to look past the symptom to the underlying reason.

All of us are motivated to do things out of our basic need to feel *significant*. Therefore, contrary to how you may feel when your child misbehaves, his goal isn't to drive you to be institutionalized. He is likely misbehaving because he feels *insignificant, inadequate, unloved,* or worse—*unlovable*.

Let me give you an example that may hit closer to home. Let's say you've established a theory that your fifth-grader goes clinically brain-dead at 3:15 P.M. Monday through Friday. Clearly there are no brainwaves because he repeatedly forgets to bring his homework home from school. Subsequently, he has done poorly on tests and receives wretched progress reports. You've scolded, swatted, taken away privileges, and even lowered worldwide parenting standards by resorting to bribery, and still the results are marginal. Momentary improvements and reason for optimism soon give way to the old patterns.

In this situation, most parents figure that since their efforts to date haven't gotten results, it's time to up the ante. They move up the line of disciplinary options, which ranges from withholding Oreos for life to house arrest. Isn't it odd that no matter what level of discipline, nothing seems to have an impact on his failure to remember to bring his homework from school?

The reason is that you as parents could not possibly conceive of a punishment that is more uncomfortable than the feelings of inadequacy that your fifth-grader's subconscious is struggling with. You see, if your child is feeling inadequate in school, *inadequate* becomes a synonym for words such as: *insignificant, insecure, fearful, helpless, hopeless,* and even *stupid.* It is entirely probable that your child does not consciously choose to forget his homework, but instead his subconscious sends him an avoidance message concerning his homework. After all, if he doesn't bring home his books, he can't study. And if he can't study, then his poor report card means he is only forgetful or lazy instead of inadequate or (worse) stupid.

Lest you go shrieking off into the darkness, ranting how I am just another one of those pointy-headed therapists who says you must never discipline your child out of fear that you will harm his little psyche—*au contraire!* Discipline, in its numerous forms, is essential to effective parenting, and a child's psyche isn't connected to his behind. What I am advocating is that before taking action, you must understand *what* is driving the misbehavior. Knowing your child's DQ Factor will help you determine that. Then, you will pick from a menu of disciplinary approaches that have been proven to work most effectively with your child's DQ Factor.

UNDERSTANDING BEFORE TAKING ACTION

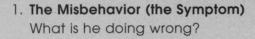

1. **The Misbehavior (the Symptom)**
   What is he doing wrong?

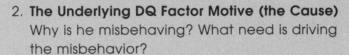

2. **The Underlying DQ Factor Motive (the Cause)**
   Why is he misbehaving? What need is driving
   the misbehavior?

3. **Taking My Child's DQ into Consideration**
   Based on the research and my child's DQ Factor, which
   disciplinary options should I consider?

4. **Taking the Right Corrective Action**
   Now that I understand the misbehavior, what (if any)
   discipline will produce the desired effect?

CHAPTER 2
MISBEHAVING FOR FUN AND PROFIT

I had barely finished a lecture on discipline when a young mother pushed her way to the podium and blurted, "My nine-year-old lies to me constantly! So what should I do? I've spanked him. I've taken away his privileges. I've even told him that I will never trust him again if he keeps lying to me. Why does he lie, and how do I make him stop?"

When asked for a recent example of catching her son in a lie, without hesitation the woman answered, "I was doing his laundry when I found a new miniature remote control car in his pants pocket. I know he has no allowance, so I asked him where he got it. He told me that he went to the store with his friend Keith and Keith's mom, and that she purchased the car for him. I knew that was not possible because Irene would have asked me before just taking him to the store. I knew he was lying."

From her expression and the tone of her voice, it was plain that this mom was completely frustrated and out of ideas as to why her son shoplifted the car and then proceeded to lie to her about it. "So what did you do next?" I asked.

"I took him to Keith's house, and I made him stand there while I asked Irene if she had taken him to the store and bought him the toy car. Of course she said she had not. Then he broke down and told me that he had ridden his bicycle to the store and had taken . . . I mean, shoplifted . . . the toy car. So why did he shoplift and then lie to me about it? And what can I do to get him to stop lying to me?"

"You ask good questions," I affirmed. "Let's start with the shoplifting question first. Then, we'll circle back and deal with the lying portion."

"Start with the knowledge that your son isn't mentally ill because he shoplifted, any more than you are a bad parent because he did so. I've met very few adults who didn't shoplift once or twice during their childhood. Remember how I described *perceived payoff* during my lecture?" I asked.

"Was that the part where you said a kid's subconscious will decide that he will risk doing X even though he may have to face Y—because X is worth the perceived payoff?" the mom responded.

"Precisely. We all do things, even though we know they are wrong, because the perceived payoff is big enough to justify the risk. Let me ask you a few questions regarding your situation with your son. First, have you taught your son that stealing is wrong?"

"Of course we have!" she protested in an insulted tone.

"Sorry, I didn't mean for you to take it the wrong way, but whenever you contemplate discipline, you have to start with the knowledge that your child was clear about breaking the rules. Okay, we've established that he knew what he was doing to be wrong, so now we can move to the issue of motive. Instead of asking yourself, 'Why did my son take the toy?' the initial question is, 'What was his perceived payoff in taking the new toy?'"

"Isn't that getting a little too deep?" the young mom inquired. "Isn't it just that he acted impulsively? He saw a cool car. He wanted it, but he didn't have any money to pay for it. I mean, isn't that just what kids do?"

"Of course it is possible," I replied. "But it is not generally that simple, and I'd be cautious not to rationalize it away as just a childhood phase. Something in either his conscious or subconscious processed through details which included *I shouldn't steal; I know this is wrong; I will get in trouble if I get caught* . . . and ended up with . . . *but this toy makes it worth taking the risk.*

"In your son's mind, something associated with having that toy (perceived payoff) made it worth the risk. Maybe it was as simple as feeling jealous that his friend had one, but the DQ Factor theory would ask you to at least consider that your son was misbehaving out of one of four areas of need. Which one (or ones) sound more likely in this situation?

"He is a DQ Factor #1—Bear who feels insignificant if he is not in control. If this is the case, he would have likely asked you for the toy car and been turned down.

"Or he is a DQ Factor #2—Monkey who feels insignificant unless he is commanding your attention, and getting into trouble was just one way of getting your attention.

"Or he is a DQ Factor #3—Porcupine who gains a sense of significance when he is getting revenge against someone who he perceives to have hurt him in some way. In this case, his revenge might have been because you wouldn't let him have the car after asking.

"Or finally, he is a DQ Factor #4—Lamb who feels insignificant and unimportant because he doesn't have a car like his friend."

Without stopping for her to choose one of the above, I continued, "Outside of sheer boredom, I've found that the motives or perceived payoffs for misbehaving have to fall into one of those four categories. It is up to you and your son to figure out which one (or combination) provided the proper motivation for him to steal."

"I see where you are going. So something about taking the toy car was so inviting that it took over his common sense and the teaching that his father and I have instilled in him. Is that it?" she inquired.

"Precisely," I complimented. "Do any of the perceived payoffs I just mentioned strike you as close to the reason that he may have shoplifted?"

Raising one eyebrow she replied, "You know what? He told me that all of his friends had come over to the house last weekend, but they didn't stay long because they were going over to another boy's house to play with their remote control cars. My son didn't go because he didn't have a car to play with. I just told him to take his old matchbox cars and he'd have just as much fun."

I allowed her time to figure out for herself what her son's likely perceived payoff was for stealing.

"So revenge over my not buying him a new toy might have been his motive. Or maybe it was that he needed to feel important with his peer group. Do those seem like possible answers, Doc?" she inquired.

"I think you are on target and that it was one of those two DQ Factors. The best way to diagnose which of the two it was is to assess *your feelings* at the time you found out about it. Your feelings are a strong truth detector in the DQ Factor puzzle. You'll find the FED-UP (Feelings Experienced During Unruly Periods) test to be very helpful in flushing out his DQ motivation," I said chuckling.

"Oh, I see. This is one of those teach-me-to-fish-by-sending-me-to-the-book versus give-me-a-fish-by-telling-me-the-answer things, huh?" she said laughing.

I just smiled.

A Concluding Thought about Perceived Payoff

Recently a couple came in for a session because their two-year-old just wouldn't behave. By the way—if you look up *two-year-old* in the dictionary, you will find a five-word definition: "exists to make you crazy."

In any event, when I asked for an example of the child's misbehavior, the mom told me that Rachel would continually pull the miniblind cords. Even after she was scolded, ushered away, or had her hand swatted, she would comply momentarily but then return for more. Theirs was a classic power-struggle ritual. To confirm the DQ Factor theory, I asked the parents, "After being scolded for touching the blinds with her hands, did Rachel ever lie on the floor and kick at the cord with her bare feet?" Both looked at each other as though I was a psychic and nodded their heads affirmatively.

You don't have to be a psychic (or a shrink) if you understand the law of perceived payoff and typical patterns of child misbehavior. Rachel was acting like a normal passive-aggressive two-year-old who found the payoff of trying to gain more (key in on the word *more*) control over her parents and receiving attention after misbehaving to be worth the scolding. The reason she lay on the floor touching the cord with her foot was because nobody told her she couldn't use her foot to touch it. She only knew for certain that touching it with her hands was off-limits. The interesting thing to note is that even though she was not using her hands to touch the cord, she still suspicioned that what she was doing was out of bounds. Still, her desire to do what she wanted (power play for control) and to get more attention outweighed her interest in following the rules. In short, Rachel's passive payoff (gaining *more* control and *more* attention) was worth taking the risk. Keep in mind that this all falls under the theory that we all, irrespective of our age, will choose to act out when we rationalize that the payoff is worth the risk.

I WANT MORE!

Without a doubt, the most problematic four-letter word that humans struggle with is *more!* And when it comes to understanding DQ Factors and discipline, you simply cannot discount the important role that *more* plays between you and your child.

A colleague recently told me of a study that focused on the *first* words uttered by toddlers. In order of frequency, they are:

#1 Mama

#2 No

#3 Dada

#4 More (which actually comes out sounding like "mo")

I'm curious about how that makes other dads feel. Not only are we in third place, we followed *no*. My unscientific hunch is this is due to all of the times our children hear their moms tell them no! They hear it directly hundreds of times a day—and they hear it directed to their fathers fairly frequently as well. I'm surprised the phrase "in your dreams, big boy" didn't hit the top four. But I digress.

If you tell your six-year-old he can't have a cookie before dinner, and yet he sneaks one when you are out of the room, there is no question that he has misbehaved. The question then becomes, Why? Did he know he wasn't supposed to take a cookie? Of course. So the next question is, Was he capable of following your no-cookie rule? Again, the answer is yes. Next, did he know that getting caught would certainly bring about consequences? Hopefully this answer is also yes, otherwise your boundaries are merely hopeful requests. (We will discuss that in later chapters.) Therefore, you must conclude that he simply chose to disobey and challenge your authority by partaking of the forbidden cookie (DQ Factor #1—Bears). His desire for *more* [cookies] was greater than his desire to follow your rules. Somewhere in his little six-year-old brain, he decided the [more] joy that a cookie creates was worth the risk of incurring your anger and any subsequent punishment.

Most of us struggle to follow the rules. We resist the temptation to make poor choices and strain to do the right thing. Still, my study into Discipline Quotients produced some fascinating facts as to why some kids persevere in doing the right thing while others quickly give in to their quest for *more*. Let me give you some examples of how *more* provides the impetus to misbehave in both children and adults. I've positioned them so as to provide a sense of how powerful *more* drives the subconscious.

❧ When a teenager disregards his mom's instruction to get off the phone and to do his homework, he just knows that it is *more* fun to talk on the phone than it is to do his homework. You, however, are now looking for the underlying motivation for his misbehavior, which is likely:

Challenging his mom's authority to tell him what to do (DQ Factor #1—Bears).

❧ A teenager threatens to run away from home because, in his mind, he wants *more* freedom. You, however, are now looking for the underlying motivation for his misbehavior, which is likely:

Attention seeking as he feels unimportant in the current family situation (DQ Factor #2—Monkeys).

❧ A child who, after begging his mom for money to buy a toy, takes ten dollars from her purse, is thinking only about how much *more* fun it will be to have a new toy. You, however, are now looking for the underlying motivation for his misbehavior, which is likely:

Revenge against his mom for keeping him from having *more* fun (DQ Factor #3—Porcupines).

❧ A teenager gets caught drinking beer at a party. He was likely doing so because he wanted to fit in and feel *more* comfortable socially. You, however, are now looking for the underlying motivation for his misbehavior, which is likely:

Defeatist in that he feels socially unacceptable and feels he can't do better without breaking his parents' rules (DQ Factor #4—Lambs).

Irrespective of the situation, the individual, or the outcome—always understand that *more* is just the symptom of the underlying motivation to misbehave.

Interestingly enough, *more* also played a major role in defining how parents desired to be seen by their children and others. Many parents were motivated in their response to their child's misbehaving by wanting to appear

- *More* in control
- *More* loving
- *More* generous
- *More* like a friend than a parent
- *More* concerned with the child's feelings than doing the right thing
- *More* accepted than the other parent
- *More* respected than the other parent
- *More* loved than the other parent

The list went on and on, but you will learn more about that later as well.

Please indulge my putting a brief biblical spin on the issue of *more* before we move forward. All of us make poor choices on an hourly basis. If you stopped long enough to analyze the reason for these poor choices, you would find the desire for *more* was likely at the root of the choice. Adam and Eve chose to eat the forbidden fruit from the tree in the Garden of Eden. Why? Because they believed that doing so, although forbidden by their Father, would give them *more* wisdom. It would allow them to be *more* like God. Perhaps it would enable them to look and feel *more* in charge of their own destiny.

Stating the obvious, it has been all downhill since then, and it remains the same today. Nothing has changed. We still want *more*. We mistakenly believe that attaining *more* of whatever it is will make us *more* significant, important, loved, and therefore happier. Needless to say, a pot of gold is seldom at the end of the *more* rainbow.

CONSULTING THE FATHERS OF PSYCHOLOGY ABOUT DQ FACTORS

A common occupational hazard to those of us who are of the psychological persuasion is that we tend to overanalyze everything. Therapists are notorious for missing the obvious by searching for some deep-seated Freudian or Pavlovian meaning that must somehow connect to how this person experienced emotional trauma at one year of age as a result of a run-in with his or her oatmeal spoon. As someone was once rumored to say to Freud, "Sometimes a cigar is just a cigar."

When it comes to the human ability to make good versus bad choices, such notables in the field of psychoanalysis as Freud, Bion, Adler, and Klein have long held to the theory that humans are morally and ethically guided by a part of the psyche referred to as the superego. It is this part of the mind that creates a desire to do and be good, avoid guilt, and even to ultimately achieve perfection. Freud, for instance, said: "The superego is the representative for us of every moral restriction, the advocate of a striving towards perfection. . . . of what is described as the higher side of human life" ("New Introductory Lectures," *Journal of Psychology* [1933]: 66).

I should make it clear that I believe Freud and his contemporaries were on target in their defining of the superego (or id)—except for its genesis (pun intended). For the most part, psychology is a godless science and therefore has blatant disregard (if not disdain) for God as the Creator. Obviously, when science is god, then God has no place in the discussion. Therefore, modern psychology holds to the belief that we traverse this daily continuum between behaving nobly and misbehaving miserably based on how well defined and managed our super-ego is. I, however, hold to the theory that God designed (and installed at the factory) a moral and ethical compass in each of us. Unlike any other creatures, humans know the difference between right (behaving) and wrong (misbehaving) and have the ability to reason through the choice. Of even greater distinction is that humans uniquely experience guilt and shame. We saw the first snapshot of this through the disobedience of Adam and Eve, who chose to break their Father's rules.

As it applies to my DQ Factor theory and to parenting, most behaviorists would agree that the cause of misbehavior among children is an inability to evaluate choices or an inability to distinguish right from wrong. The area of research that I ventured into, and hope will inspire others to follow, centers not with *how* kids misbehave, but *what* inspires and motivates them to misbehave. So while other behaviorists might look at a misbehaving child or teen and address an underevolved superego that allows for misbehavior, I look at the motivation driving the misbehavior.

Perhaps the person who came closest to my DQ Factor theory was a relatively obscure therapist by the name of Rudolph Dreikurs, who studied and wrote extensively on the subject of childhood antisocial and antagonistic behavior. Dreikurs's work was incredible, but it did not extend much past misbehaving motives among children. Knowing what drives misbehavior in our children is essential, but learning various discipline techniques and their probability of success is a breakthrough.

Another more well-known therapist, Abraham Maslow, developed some tremendous theories on man's hierarchy of needs. Maslow believed that for man to achieve self-actualization (true happiness and fulfillment), he must have his most basic needs met.

Maslow's hierarchy of needs starts with *physiological needs* such as food, water, and air. The second level of need is for *safety*, categorized roughly as security; stability; dependency; protection; freedom from fear, anxiety, and chaos; need for structure, order, law, and limits; strength in the protector.

The third in his five levels to self-actualization is *belongingness* and *love needs*.

If both the physiological and the safety needs are fairly well met, the feelings of love, affection, and belonging that are needed to be truly happy will emerge. These involve giving and receiving affection, and when they are unsatisfied, a person will feel keenly the absence of friends, mate, or children. Such a person will hunger for relations with people in general—for a place in the group or family—and will strive with great intensity to achieve this goal. Attaining such a place will matter more than anything else in the world, and he or she may even forget that at one time, when hunger was foremost, love seemed unreal, unnecessary, and unimportant. Now the pangs of loneliness, ostracism, rejection, and friendlessness are preeminent.

Esteem is the fourth level of the hierarchy. This is the level that comes the closest to describing motivations driving misbehavior, thus supporting the evidence I discovered during my DQ study.

All people in our society (with a few pathological exceptions) have a need or desire for a stable, firmly based, usually high evaluation of themselves—for self-respect or self-esteem. These needs may therefore be classified into two subsidiary sets. These are, first, the desire for strength, achievement, adequacy, mastery and competence, confidence in the face of the world, and independence and freedom. Second, we have what we may call the desire for reputation or prestige (defining it as "respect or esteem from other people"): status, fame and glory, dominance, recognition, attention, importance, dignity, or appreciation. Satisfaction of the self-esteem need leads to feelings of self-confidence, worth, strength, capability, and adequacy, of being useful and necessary in the world. But thwarting of these needs produces feelings of inferiority, weakness, and helplessness.

As Maslow clearly noted, the human drive to feel important, significant, and held in high regard is critical not only to one's happiness, but also to one's overall mental health. I concur with his theory and found it equally relevant in evaluating the reasons that drive our conscious misbehavior.

Maslow's final level of self-actualization rested in the theory that even if we are happy in all of the other areas, if we are not doing what we individually are fitted for, then we will not truly be happy. I think Maslow was on target with this premise, yet I find it amusing that he never gave credit where credit is due—to God and the Bible. Whereas Maslow pointed out that musicians must make music, artists must paint, and poets must write if they are to be ultimately at peace with themselves, he never connected it to the *spiritual gifts* mentioned often in the Bible, or to the fact that God Himself holds us responsible to use our spiritual gifts in order to attain real contentedness.

All right, enough psychobabble from the masters of psychology. Let's move on to understanding your child's misbehaving motivations.

Misbehaving 101

At the risk of breaking some heavy news to you here, (gasp) every child acts out! Every kid creates at least an occasional discipline challenge to his or her parents. As far back as time records, children have caused their parents to pull their hair out. In fact, a little perspective is sometimes a powerful thing. The next time you get your undies in a giant knot because your six-year-old stashed a Twinkie under his mattress, peruse the first book of the Bible. We touched on it a few pages back, but each of us remembers the story of Adam and Eve and how they ate the forbidden fruit that God had warned them about. That's right—God started the human race with two misbehaving kids—of sorts. In fact, in ancient Hebrew, the word *genesis* translates to: Get ready because your kids are going to challenge you until your hair turns gray and falls out in clumps.

And no way did the acting out and parental challenge stop with Adam and Eve. Remember, the Bible is very clear on this whole principle of *reaping what you sow*: You know—if you do this, then that will happen. Why didn't God just call it *payback*? Wouldn't it have been a clearer warning to parents if He had just come right out and told us that if you were a rotten little firestarter as a kid, then produce offspring at your own risk? If you read a little farther in Genesis, to chapter 3, you'll note that Adam and Eve had two sons (as if that wasn't punishment enough) named Cain and Abel. Let the record reflect that those two set an all-time (granted, time was limited back then) low for conduct unbecoming to offspring. In case you don't recall the story (or a Bible is only something you use to crush spiders with in a motel room), Cain ended up murdering Abel. So the next time you have an out-of-body experience because your son forgot to put down the toilet seat when he finished his business, perhaps you should harken back to when you were a kid and wonder if this is God's little inside joke, affectionately called *payback!*

CHAPTER 3
THE REMARKABLE DQ FACTOR STUDY

While I was in graduate school, one of my professors took a particular interest in my research into child and teenage conduct disorders within single-parent families. He found it particularly interesting that my experience as a police officer had provided me with a vastly different and expanded perspective into child and adolescent *mis*behavior than that of my fellow shrinks-to-be.

My professor suggested I study the work of a particular therapist, Salvador Minuchin. Minuchin, like Maslow, was one of the "giants" who founded the concept of family therapy back in the 1950s. He saw the family as a system with a structure that tended to be self-maintaining under changing internal and external conditions. According to Minuchin, some family systems are dysfunctional in that they produce and perpetuate suffering on the part of the members of the family. His solution was to change the family system (from inside the family) in order to restore healthy functioning through the encouragement of certain principles such as hierarchy (parents in charge), boundaries, avoidance of scapegoating individual family members, avoidance of conversational triangles, and so on.

My professor thought that Minuchin's unusual method—he physically lived with and observed families in order to get a firsthand view of the family dysfunction before, during, and after discipline problems—would be beneficial. Minuchin's theory was that only by infiltrating the family in motion could he truly understand the family dynamics. He had a valid point, but I wasn't about to ask 147 families if I could move in with them for the summer. Instead, I instructed the survey participants in the fine art of journaling.

The problem with journaling their thoughts, feelings, and emotions as soon as possible following a misbehavior and a disciplinary conflict was that it afforded family members time to calm down and to process their feelings and emotions. What I received was far too cleaned up and rational. If I was going to truly understand the feelings and emotions that both parent and child experience during, and immediately following, a conflict, I would need to be an eyewitness—or at least the next closest thing to it. Following the Minuchin model (with a slight technological adjustment), I relied instead on audio- and videotape recorders to become my eyes and ears among my 147 volunteer families.

I made one primary request of the participating families and one specific request of the parent(s). The first request was to try to ignore the presence of audio- and video-recording equipment and to function as *normally* as possible. An additional request of the parents concerned the need to complete a task immediately following any of their child's misbehaviors. I asked them to record their thoughts, emotions, and the outcome surrounding the entire conflict. To facilitate this essential aspect of my overall study, I coached each parent in what I needed and prepared a ten-question prompt sheet to solicit the recorded information.

To say I was pleasantly surprised with how quickly the families got into the routine of turning on (and then forgetting about) the recorders prior to their morning, after-school, and evening rituals would be a gross understatement. With very few exceptions, each of the families went about their normal day-to-day activities. It seemed that each was initially cognizant of the recording equipment but soon fell into their routine seemingly unfazed by my intrusion. The evidence of this could be found in sensitive and private (even sexual) conversations and inappropriate language at times. By nature, the fact that several families said mean-spirited things, called each other unflattering names, or did inappropriate things was evidence that they had forgotten my electronic intrusion and were back to their routine. The results were truly amazing as well as psychologically significant.

IN SEARCH OF KNOWLEDGE

As a researcher into human behavior, it is always important to have a goal firmly in mind prior to starting any significant research project. In all research, it is essential that the goal not be confused with an outcome. The goals of this project were the following:

GOAL #1: To study a statistically significant number of families in order to identify potential patterns among children and teenagers as to why and how they misbehave.

GOAL #2: To explore the possibility that these patterns might lead to discovering misbehaving types or specific DQ Factors among children and teenagers.

GOAL #3: If, in fact, DQ Factor groups were established among children and teens, then explore ways of creating a simple system enabling parents to evaluate their own children to establish which DQ Factor(s) they gravitate toward.

GOAL #4: Once a parent established his or her child's DQ Factor(s), then create an awareness about that Factor in parents so that they can identify the warning signs that lead to misbehavior in their child before it happens.

GOAL #5: To provide parents with a matrix of proactive and responsive disciplinary techniques that have been statistically proven most effective in curtailing future misbehaviors.

GOAL #6: To teach parents to identify their own issues (confrontational, enmeshed, permissive, etc.) that often lead to heightened conflicts between a parent and a particular DQ Factor child.

The object of my study into the existence of DQ Factors among children, teens, and parents was never to impress clinicians or to end up in the journals of psychiatry and psychology. To do so would have meant publishing thousands of pages of statistical analysis, hypotheses, outcome analyses, and enough clinical jargon to create hundreds of new narcolepsy cases. My past experience in going through the psychological gymnastics of publishing studies taught me that it is not worth the time, energy, or resources. It is far more rewarding to target the people who stand to gain the most from this knowledge—parents.

Eavesdropping on 147 Families Isn't Easy, but It Is Entertaining

By networking several groups of therapists, pediatricians, and social workers, I was able to gather 147 volunteer families who agreed to participate in my study. The study commenced on October 2, 1999, and spanned nearly sixteen months, when all the follow-up was complete. In spite of the sizable task of working with so many subjects, the request I made of each family was relatively simple. I asked the parent(s) of each of the 147 families to record all significant interactions they had with their children during certain hours of the day. Since the average family spent approximately 1.7 hours together on weekdays and 2.3 hours together on weekends, I found that one six-hour cassette tape generally did the trick. In addition, I asked sixteen of the families to use both video-and audiotape during their prime parent-child interactions. The benefit of using a video camera was to gain a better understanding of nonverbal signals that accompanied verbal confrontations.

Here is a breakdown of the participating families:

TOTAL: 147 FAMILIES

82 Caucasian families

18 African-American families

23 Asian families

24 Hispanic families

62 teenagers (between the ages of 13 and 18)

85 children (between the ages of 5 and 12)

109 moms and dads (currently in two-parent unit families)

33 single moms (divorced with joint custody)

5 single dads (divorced with joint custody)

Because our study spanned sixteen months, we staff members started feeling like we were part of the participating families. There was also a luxury afforded us that no other known study had ever accomplished: We were able to observe family cycles from one year into the next.

BEWARE OF THE HIGH-RISK WEEK

The first order of business was to gather the audio- and videotapes accumulated over the sixteen months. Next, along with more than twenty interns, I listened to and interpreted the tapes and then compiled a statistical chart based on every aspect of every disagreement, altercation, misbehaving episode, discipline issue, and resolution. As is often the case, a statistical trend began to evolve.

Shortly thereafter, an *algorithm* (really cool scientific word that means a predictable mathematical pattern used to solve problems) began to emerge, foretelling such matters as the day of week and time of day that families were statistically more likely to encounter challenges. For instance, we noted a pattern between husbands and wives that seemed to take place like clockwork. Whenever we monitored tapes bearing a label for the twenty-fifth of any month and continuing through the end of the month, we noted an 18 percent increase in tension, arguments, and temper outbursts between spouses. We also noticed a 17 percent increase in alcohol consumption during the final five days of each month, coupled with a 22 percent increase in consumption of over-the-counter medicines including aspirin, sleep aids, and stomachache relief formulas. Tapes from the last week of each month were also 26 percent more likely to reveal some significant behavioral problems among children and teens.

Our curiosity demanded that we examine every possible reason as to why there was so much more stress-related activity associated with the last week of the month. We charted items as obscure as lunar and tidal patterns. We looked at barometric pressures and other weather-related patterns. But when no observable evidence surfaced for these changes, we had to look deeper into the family system.

I found the answer to the increase in month's-end tension on my own kitchen table. Coming home on the evening of March 26, I asked my wife if we'd received any mail. She handed me envelopes containing bills ranging from the ones for the phones to my son's missing retainer (presumably abandoned on a school cafeteria tray, although he is sticking to the story that our Australian shepherd ate it). Thumbing my way through the car repair bill, the vet bill for Ruthy the golden retriever's thyroid condition (the dog is a stress eater), the gasoline and other assorted credit cards, mortgage and car payments, the electric bill, and property taxes was enough to make me shriek and run to the pharmacy for some aspirin and Pepto Bismol too. Our study of these families revealed that, as in my own family, 38 percent of parental and head-of-household stress is concentrated in the final 25 percent of the month.

It's completely logical when you think about it. If the month is divided equally into four weekly pieces comprising 25 percent each, then each week should carry an equal amount (or 25 percent) of life's pressures. But, when you factor in month-end financial obligations, work-related deadlines, and the tension of the depleting family budget, then it is much easier to understand why the fourth week of the month carries 38 percent of the stress load.

We also found that children under the age of twelve were 22 percent more likely to break a significant family rule between the twenty-fifth and the end of each month. Whether it was sneaking out of the house while on restriction, breaking curfew, or shoplifting, it was simply more likely to happen during those final seven days. The rationale is that families are connected emotionally. Simply put, whenever tensions (of any sort) permeate the home, kids will pick up on it. Even if the stressors are never discussed, children will see and feel the changes.

We made a second noteworthy observation pertaining to how children and teenagers reacted to stressed-out parents. Moms and dads handled their stress in various ways. Some seemed to manage it well. With these parents, it was actually difficult to tell if they were having a good day or a bad day. They seemed to relate to, and interact with, their children in a consistent manner, irrespective of their moods.

A second group of parents withdrew and became sullen and moody when faced with their stressors. We noted that their children were prone to emotional outbursts and other attention-seeking misbehaviors. We all recognize that most kids and teens have little or no vocabulary for asking their parents what is wrong or if the tension is about them. They also do not have a vocabulary to request what they need emotionally. This includes asking their parents for more attention. As a result, the kids simply misbehave to get it. For instance, we observed that these kids would become huge nuisances during these times. They would whine, bicker, throw tantrums—in short, anything they could do to get their parents' attention. Even if the attention was negative, it was still attention.

A third group of parents allowed their stressors to dictate their moods in the opposite direction from those who withdrew. They would engage the other members of the family in angry, short-tempered, and even mean-spirited ways. This was how these parents tried to appease their moods. Their ineffective methods had a doubly deleterious effect on their children. Even though you could say that at least the kids were receiving attention, it was angry and punitive. As a result, these children often became actively rebellious, angry, confrontational, and even looked for ways to get back at their parents for the way their parents made them feel.

The information and statistical support concerning the final week of each month was so compelling that I decided to expand my research. Drawing on my law-enforcement background, I checked with an ex-colleague in the U.S. Justice Department's National Incident-Based Reporting System (NIBRS), and my friend was able to produce statistics that actually validated (on a national scale) what we had observed in our study. As suspected, the following crimes showed a significant increase during the final week of each month:

REPORTED INCIDENT	PERCENTAGE FOR THE MONTH DURING THE FINAL WEEK
Shoplifting among juveniles	28%
Shoplifting among children	29%

REPORTED INCIDENT	PERCENTAGE FOR THE MONTH DURING THE FINAL WEEK
Shoplifting among adults (female)	33%
Shoplifting among adults (male)	39%
Drunk driving among teenagers (female)	29%
Drunk driving among teenagers (male)	33%
Family disturbance calls	37%
Runaway minors (12 yrs. and younger—female)	27%
Runaway minors (12 yrs. and younger—male)	29%
Runaway minors (13 yrs. to 18 yrs.—female)	29%
Runaway minors (13 yrs. to 18 yrs.—male)	32%
Misdemeanor assault (husband upon wife)	32%
Misdemeanor assault (wife upon husband)	28%
Child abuse reports (mother upon child)	24%
Child abuse reports (father upon child)	29%
Drunk in public (male adults)	35%
Drunk in public (female adults)	29%

Put your personal family experience to the test. See if you can determine a specific time in the month that produces more stress and, therefore, more family tensions and arguments.

OBSERVING RISK ELEMENTS IN DAILY ROUTINES

By cross-referencing the above statistics with our own research, we not only proved that families are statistically more likely to experience problems during the final week of each month, but that it was possible to counteract this occurrence.

An undeniable truth in life is that knowledge is power. Let me give you an example. We approached a group of twenty-five families for the express purpose of equipping them with the knowledge that the final 25 percent of each month produces 35 to 40 percent of the stress. We tested the theory that informing each parent of the fourth-week stress factor could reduce the incidence of family conflict and its accompanying misbehavior among siblings. Our theory was quickly proven to be correct. Among those twenty-five families, 68 percent of them were able to reduce conflicts simply by focusing their attention on that seven-day high-risk time period.

A problem we discovered shortly thereafter was that the benefit was short-lived. Although we were able to establish that providing information to parents was immediately beneficial in lowering conflicts, long-term and lasting change had to come through education and providing tools for improvement. This was demonstrated as we noted most of the twenty-five families slipping back into their familiar patterns as soon as their focus returned to their usual problems. Industrial psychologists (those who practice and apply psychology in the workplace) have long held that focusing one's attention on any problem, even without additional training or tools, will bring about change. The challenge has always been one of holding on to the change.

We conducted a second control group study with an additional twenty-five parents. In addition to informing these parents of the stress factors associated with the last week of each month, we also taught them modest stress-reduction and coping techniques. For instance, we started with proper diet, exercise, and sleep suggestions. We taught them the basics of biofeedback, including techniques that would allow them to feel and monitor their stress levels prior to losing control. And finally, we asked them to talk as a family about the financial stress they felt instead of bottling it up. We even suggested they provide their children and teenagers with age-appropriate information concerning the weekly and monthly budgets so as to foster a sense of cooperation. All in all, the training took less than three hours per family, and the results were staggering. Among the control group parents, month-end conflicts were reduced by 52 percent.

CHOOSING YOUR FAVORITE CONFLICT DU JOUR

After developing and proving our observations pertaining to the most stressful time of the month, we turned our attention to discovering the troublesome daily routines.

The purpose of this portion of the study was to identify a list of routines—tasks, chores, and responsibilities—that often feature misbehaving among children and teens and frustration among parents. Each task, chore, or responsibility has been ranked with a number. The number represents the frequency in which both children and teenagers seized the moment to act out in some form of misbehavior. Here is how the list shaped up:

PROBLEMATIC WEEKDAY ROUTINES	MISBEHAVING RANKING
MORNING	
Waking up on time	#1
Waking up on own	#2
Getting out the door on time	#3
Getting dressed in a timely fashion	#4
Getting breakfast prepared and eaten in a timely fashion	#5
Getting dressed in appropriate attire	#6

PROBLEMATIC WEEKDAY ROUTINES	MISBEHAVING RANKING
Getting ready for school (work for parents)	#7
Hunting for misplaced/lost items needed for that day	#8
AFTERNOON	
After-school activities (soccer, scouting, etc.)	#1
Not doing homework	#2
Creating messes	#3
Forgetting needed items from school (homework, books, notes, etc.)	#4
Forgetting or not doing chores	#5
Getting ready for dinner	#6
DINNER AND BEDTIME	
Starting or completing homework	#1
After-school activities (sports, clubs, lessons)	#2
Dinner together (conversations, problems from the day)	#3
Getting ready for dinner (putting away things and cleaning up)	#4
After-dinner cleanup	#5
Getting ready for bed (brushing teeth, baths, etc.)	#6
Getting kids to go to bed when told	#7
Getting kids to stay in bed through the night	#8
Kids stalling or refusing to turn off TV/stereo or hang up phone	#9

PROBLEMATIC WEEKDAY ROUTINES	MISBEHAVING RANKING
Pre-bedtime activities (bath, shower, brushing teeth)	#10
Bed-wetting	#11

Remember, these were compilations of typical activities that go on in homes on a daily basis. This opportunities to misbehave menu likely matches your own family experiences. Don't worry if the numerical misbehavior rankings differ from yours; the real value comes from understanding the setting and the risk factor. The benefit of identifying these actions is to equip you with knowledge so that you may avoid the pitfalls of the families from our study.

You will learn more about how to handle high-risk situations in later chapters.

DROPPING IN ON "MARRIED WITH CHILDREN"

When you listen to and view hundreds of tapes, sheer boredom forces you to find ways to enliven the process. For instance, we found ourselves tagging certain families with pseudonyms such as the Cunninghams (based on the 1970s sitcom *Happy Days*), Ozzie and Harriet, or one of my favorite families, the Munsters. Even though we recognized that applying labels to many of the families could evoke a modicum of bias, none of the monikers was mean-spirited or disruptive to an honest evaluation of their individual circumstances. Besides . . . it was fun.

Along these lines, it was a fascinating study in human behavior to watch my team of interns as they listened to the tapes and gained insights into the anonymous families participating in the study. One of the most revealing aspects of the study, from a human-interest perspective, was seen in how quickly the team identified the patterns of families. For instance, upon checking in one afternoon, one intern—Josie—picked up the previous week's tapes for Family #44.

Demonstrating just how little it takes to amuse psychologists (and their interns), I overheard Josie say, "Alrighty then . . . I have my snack items and my bottle of water . . . and now it's time to tune into this week's thrill-packed episode of *Married with Children.* You may recall that last week we left the somewhat controlling Peg Bundy and her lovable yet dysfunctional husband, Al, as they were discussing how to deal with young Bud (not the sharpest crayon in the box) and his miserable report card. As memory serves, Peg and Al were debating whether to ground Bud for thirty-seven years, or shave his head, or both. Let's check in on Family #44, shall we?"

In her own way, Josie characterized how familiar we had become with the families we were monitoring, considering that over the span of several months, we dealt with a few hundred tapes and thousands of pages of transcripts. Some, if not most of the families, became very predictable. By predictable, I mean that very clear-cut patterns emerged not only within the individual families, but among the group of families as well.

Let me provide you with a prime example from several volumes of tapes of the Leonard family.

THE LEONARDS

PARENTS
Mom: Irene
Dad: Donald

CHILDREN
Dustin (age 13)
Darin (age 11)
Donna (age 7)

Tape #28, which was later characterized as "Darin's Disastrous Report Card Debacle," featured some great before-dinner dialogue between Darin and his parents. It seemed that the sixth-grader had completely caught his parents off guard by bringing home a progress report indicating he was receiving D's and low C's in each academic class because of poor homework habits. The angry discourse between Darin and his parents was transcribed and served to illustrate just how ineffective we parents can be when we launch into Disciplinary Factor dialogue without any specific outcome in mind. Here are the highlights:

MOM   *"I simply cannot believe you! This is just . . . unbelievable."*

DAD   *"I can't believe you either!"* (silence for 30 seconds)

DARIN   *"Mrs. Embersol says I haven't turned in all my homework, which is why my grades aren't as good."*

MOM   *"Do you mean to sit there and tell me that you are failing the sixth grade because you are not turning in your homework again? Why do you put us through the same thing year after year after year?"*

DAD   *"That's a fair question, Darin. Whose fault is it that you don't do your homework? Is it my fault? Is it your mom's fault? Maybe it was Danielle's fault. Whose fault was it, Darin?"* (38 seconds pass)

MOM   *"We're waiting."* (39 seconds pass)

DAD   *"We're still waiting, son. We've tried everything imaginable to help you to do better in school and to do your homework, and you still bring home grades that should make you ashamed of yourself. What do you have to say?"* (22 seconds pass)

         "What is it going to take for you to finally start doing what we and your teacher tell you to do?" (30 seconds pass) *"Well?"*

DARIN	*"It's just that I don't have time to do my homework at school. Everyone else has study period as their fifth-period class, but I have to go to soccer practice."*
DAD	*"Why is it that Dustin can do his schoolwork just fine? He has just as many soccer practices and games as you do, but he seems to be able to get it done. Do you mean to tell me that every other player on your soccer team is failing the sixth grade because they aren't turning in their homework?"*
DARIN	*"Not everyone, but almost everyone says the same thing. Even Mrs. Embersol says I'm one of her best students, but I don't have time to study and to do my homework, so my grades stink."*
MOM	*"I'll tell you one thing that is going to change right now, mister. Starting tomorrow, you are grounded. And I'm not talking for just a week or two. Starting tomorrow, you will come home right after soccer and you WILL have your homework and your books in your backpack. You'll go right to your room and you will study. Then we will go through your homework every night. Is that clear?"* (10 seconds pass)
DAD	*"And I think we should enroll him at Sylvan as his teacher suggested last time. Then he will have somewhere to do his homework and someone to help who knows what his teacher is looking for. Would that be helpful, Darin?"*
DARIN	*"I don't know. I'm not going to that Sylvan place. That's for stupid kids, and I'm not going."*
DAD	*"That's insane. You need the help, and you are not the one in charge of who does what in this house. When you hit eighteen you can decide what you do, but until then, you follow our rules. And you can forget about television watching in your room. As of right now, the TV is off-limits. Do you read me?"*
DARIN	*"Yeah."*

To illustrate my point of how families become stuck in dysfunctional cycles of misbehavior—followed by ineffective discipline—followed by the same misbehavior again, take a look at the following dialogue. This tape again featured the Leonard family, but was recorded nearly six months later.

MOM   (At the dinner table with family present) *"Donald, Darin got some pretty bad news today about his grades. I can't believe after all the times we have been through this that he would continue to neglect his homework, but Mrs. Embersol sent home a note on his progress report that basically said he is missing more than a dozen assignments. He is still not turning in his homework."*

DAD   *"What is wrong with you, Darin? I mean it . . . what is wrong with you? It is either that you don't listen or you don't care. Which one is it?"* (silence for 25 seconds)

DARIN   *"Mrs. Embersol lost my essay and one of my book reports. But I thought I was doing a lot better."*

MOM   *"Well, apparently you are the only one who thinks you are doing better! Why can't you turn in your homework? Why do we have to go through this month after month? We don't have this problem with Dustin. Why do you think that is?"*

DAD   *"That's a fair question, Darin. Why do you think that Dustin is able to do his homework and you can't? He has soccer. He has just as much to do as you, but he seems to get it done. Why is that?"* (38 seconds pass)

MOM   *"We're waiting."* (39 seconds pass)

DARIN   *"I don't know."*

DAD   *"'I don't know' doesn't cut it. We've tried everything with you! You should be ashamed of yourself. What do you have to say?"* (30 seconds pass) *"Well?"*

DARIN   "I don't know. It's just that I don't have time to do my homework at school like all the other guys on my team. Then by the time I get home from soccer practice or a game, it's dinnertime and then I am too tired."

DAD   "It's the same old story. Every other player on your soccer team has time to do his homework, but somehow you are the only one who can't turn it in, right?"

DARIN   "Well, not everyone. R. J. has trouble, too, but his parents don't yell at him."

MOM   "We're not R. J.'s parents and I'll bet that if I called R. J.'s mom, she'd tell me that R. J.'s grades are just as much a problem for them as your grades are for us."

DAD   "I'll tell you one thing that is going to change right now, mister. Starting tomorrow, you're grounded for the rest of the school year. Starting tomorrow, you'll come home right after soccer with all your homework assignments and your books. You'll go right to your room and study. Is that clear?" (30 seconds pass)

DARIN   "Yeah."

DAD   (to wife) "And another thing. I think you should take Darin down to Sylvan tomorrow and see if they have an after-school homework assistance program. That way, rather than sitting in his room after dinner watching television, he can be doing his homework."

DARIN   "I'm not going to moron camp after school to do my homework."

DAD   "When you hit eighteen and you show that you have good enough judgment to do your schoolwork, then maybe you can have a say in what you do. Until then, as long as you live under my roof, you'll do as you are told. Do you read me?"

DARIN   "Yeah."

Summary

I'm sure you noticed that not much changed. Even though some six months had elapsed between the two conversations, Darin and his parents were still battling the same school and homework problem. You might also notice that Mom and Dad demonstrated poor follow-through. They threatened their son with restriction, no television, and going to Sylvan Learning Center. Clearly, none of these came to fruition or lasted over the long haul.

Darin's family is a classic example of the dysfunctional cycle that commonly occurs between a DQ Factor #1—Bear, who challenges his parents' authority. In this case, Darin figured out that his parents made idle threats that they didn't follow through on. He had discovered, over time, that if he put up a challenge by refusing to do something, they would eventually derail and forget about it.

We will take a much more in-depth look at each of the specific DQ Factor types in subsequent chapters.

CHAPTER 4
WANTED: ZOOKEEPER

Like most doctors and researchers, I tend to think too much in cold, clinical terms. This was the case throughout my DQ Factor study. As I began writing, however, I tried to keep foremost in my mind that moms and dads would be reading this book. Having written several books for parents, as well as educational products for students and teachers, I thought this book would present no greater task. This seemed to be the case up to the moment when my wife read the headings I was using for the various DQ Factor types. Our conversation went something like this:

MY WIFE   *"Are you going to refer to each of the DQ Factor types as DQ/C, DQ/R, DQ/A and the like?"*

ME   *"I suppose so. I mean, the Meyers-Briggs people haven't done too poorly with their EMTJ nomenclature. And since I'm stacking DQ Factor up with the Stanford Binet IQ tests and the Meyers-Briggs personality inventories, I thought it would be fitting that I use labels like DQ/C."*

MY WIFE   *"I understand your point. Were you planning on selling this book to other shrinks, or were you planning on selling this book to moms and dads?"*

ME   *"Since you and I both know that, throughout the entire universe, there is only one psychologist who actually buys a book, and then he loans it to every other psychologist, then I guess parents are the target audience."*

MY WIFE   *"Then speaking as a mom, I'd be put off by the reference that my kids are DQ/C's or DQ/X,Y,Z's."*

ME   *"You are probably right* [note qualified agreement technique learned in first year of marriage]. *What do you suggest?"*

MY WIFE   *"I'd suggest you refer to them as animals such as lambs or monkeys so that parents can identify with them."*

ME   *"You are right, dear!"* (Note—dropped the qualifying word "probably" and just agreed. Technique learned in second year of marriage.)

So with my wife's blessing, I assembled a small group of parents to serve as a focus group. Their task was to come up with animal types that most closely resembled my DQ Factor types. After several days the parents developed a laundry list of animals ranging from aardvarks to yaks. After much deliberation, we collectively arrived at the following animals to correspond with their DQ Factor labels:

DQ Factor #1—Bears
DQ Factor #2—Monkeys
DQ Factor #3—Porcupines
DQ Factor #4—Lambs

With that said, I'd like to be the first to welcome you to your own DQ Factor zoo. Your new official title is zookeeper. Perhaps you've always sensed that was your role in the family anyway.

Why Do We Misbehave?

Throughout the family studies, I identified nearly two hundred different ways that kids and teenagers act out or misbehave. Think about this topic from your own experience as a parent. Our kids will never run out of ways to misbehave. At age five, my son thought it would be cute to give our German shepherd a mohawk. The dog, I'm certain, felt otherwise, although she went along with it. Your child might choose to display his displeasure by carving his initials in the windowsill or even running away from home. I'm not sure there is enough time and paper in the world to list the ways kids and teens can misbehave.

The more interesting phenomenon, however, is that in spite of hundreds of symptoms (the ways kids misbehave) there were really only four *rationales* (or *underlying motives*) that we could pinpoint for *why* they misbehaved. You may recall our earlier look at Abraham Maslow and his hierarchy of needs. The simple truth is that most (although some will argue all) behavior is designed to make us feel more important, more significant, and that we belong. The DQ Factor study revealed that children, teens, and many adults often embark on a misguided adventure of doing or saying the wrong thing (misbehaving) out of their need to feel more important, significant, or that they belong. It isn't that these goals are not essential—they absolutely are to a healthy life. It is, however, the counterfeit method of achieving them that causes the problems. Therefore, the key to understanding any misbehavior is to first understand the rationale (or motivation) behind it.

RATIONALE 101

Nearly all dictionaries define *rationale* using such terms as the underlying reason, explanation, or justification. As you delve deeper into my DQ Factor theory, it would be helpful to keep in mind that all forms of purposeful (even subconscious) misbehavior are symptoms of some deeper need. Whether the misbehavior is done to challenge authority, gain sympathy, command attention, or exact revenge, it is just that person's rationalized attempt at trying to get to the true goal—

to feel significant, to feel loved, and to belong.

Let me give you a recent example. I was called in for a consultation with a teacher regarding a fourth-grader who insisted on shouting out answers to questions the teacher would pose to the class. The teacher patiently counseled the little girl to raise her hand and wait to be called upon, but that approach didn't work. She tried time-outs while the other kids were at recess, but that didn't work either. The teacher thought she finally had the answer when she told the girl that she would send her to the principal's office if she blurted out the answer without being called upon. Sure enough, the annoyance continued. Principal, here we come.

I invited the little girl's mom and dad and teacher for a strategic meeting. Each came in with a cooperative spirit of doing whatever needed to be done to help. After verifying that the fourth-grader was not coping with any emotional or psychological challenges that would override her impulse control, I was ready to move to the rationale for her behavior.

Turning my attention first to the parents, I asked, "All families place different weight and value on grades, participation, and school performance. In your home, how would you characterize the importance of class participation and getting good grades?"

Without hesitation, Mom answered, "It is something we learned the hard way, Doctor. Christina has an older brother, David, who is three grades ahead. He has not had an easy time of it in school . . ."

"That's not exactly fair," the dad interrupted. "I don't know if it is so much that he has not had an easy time in school versus his lack of effort. He is just one of these kids who slacks off and gets by with doing the minimum."

Likely moving in the right direction, I asked, "And what, if anything, has Christina seen of her older brother's struggles in school?"

"Oh, she's seen it all!" Mom replied. "She's seen the temper tantrums at the kitchen table. She's seen the notes come home that he wasn't trying in class. She's been aware of the parent-teacher conferences . . . she's seen it all."

"Can you tell me what sort of limits or consequences Christina has seen you and your husband place on her older brother as a result of school problems?" I asked.

Looking first at his wife and then at me, Christina's dad spoke first. "I know for a fact that she was upset when we took him out of the public school and sent him to a private school."

"May I make the leap of assuming that he used to attend the same school your daughter is currently attending?" I inquired.

"Yes, he did. In fact, he had Ms. Moyer too," he said, nodding his head in the direction of Christina's teacher. "We blessed Ms. Moyer with not just one, but two of our little darlings," he concluded with a smile.

"And what do you remember Christina asking or saying when her brother was transferred to the other school?"

Chiming in, Mom responded, "She was upset and at first thought David had been kicked out of school by Ms. Moyer and the administration."

"So, it is reasonable to believe that Christina is suffering under the false belief that her brother was kicked out of school because he didn't participate or do well in class?"

"Yes," both parents replied simultaneously. "I suppose that is the conclusion she would have drawn."

"Then my sense is that Christina may be suffering with anxiety about how she performs in school and her ability to demonstrate her participation and intelligence."

"I'm not sure I follow, Doc," Christina's dad admitted.

"Let's start with the understanding that Christina is misbehaving in class. When Ms. Moyer corrects Christina, it is still not enough to get her to stop disrupting the class by blurting out the answer before being called upon. Are we all together?" I asked.

All three nodded their heads.

Continuing down the path, I stated, "Then we can assume that Christina has centered on a behavior—in this case, answering questions out loud before being called on—because it serves a purpose. Even though she is aware that she is getting into trouble for doing so, what it provides her justifies the risk. So the question I would pose to the three of you is, what is Christina's *payoff* or *benefit* in continuing to misbehave in class?"

Christina's mom was the first with the answer. "She gets to convince Ms. Moyer and her dad and me that she is smart and that she is trying hard in school."

"Yes!" I commended. "Very good. And on top of that, she is trying to separate herself from her brother, and as such, won't receive the same consequences he faced. Plus, at an even deeper subconscious level, Christina is probably trying to convince herself that she is smart and therefore safe from being taken from her familiar school environment."

"So then . . . what are you saying?" Christina's dad asked with a puzzled expression.

"What I'm suggesting is that we acknowledge that Christina has adopted a conduct problem out of a legitimate need. Even at the risk of getting into trouble in class, she sees the trade-off for misbehaving as worth the risk."

Ms. Moyer spoke for the first time. "You mentioned payoff a moment ago. What do you think Christina's ultimate goal is?"

"Really, her goals are not any different than any of ours. We want to feel safe, to belong, and to feel significant. When Christina sits silently in her seat, she doesn't feel safe because that is what she perceived landed her brother in another school. She doesn't feel she belongs because of how tentative she experiences school through her brother's transfer. And finally, she seeks a feeling of significance in school (*I answer questions, so therefore I am smart*) in hopes of being good enough to belong."

After a moment of pondering and silence, Christina's mom said, "I completely understand what you are saying, and I believe you are correct. But how do we change her misbehaving and talking out of turn in class?"

"That's the right question," I commended. "But the first order of business is to see her misbehaving as just a symptom of the true problem. The symptom is that Christina is blurting out answers in class. The symptom tells us that she is feeling insecure in school and that she thinks that by commanding attention, she will achieve security by appearing smart and participative. Therefore, the underlying question to examine is, How do we make Christina feel more secure in school? Once you address this, then the symptoms generally take care of themselves."

With a hint of impatience, Christina's dad asked, "So our next step would be . . . ?"

"Your next step would be for each of you, including Ms. Moyer, to set out a well-defined routine that will communicate to Christina that she is *safe* in her classroom, that she *belongs* in her school, and that she is *significant* to her teacher, classmates, and to both of you."

With that, we devised a program whereby Christina's mom helped out in the classroom one afternoon a week. This was done so that Christina would feel that her family was more involved and invested in her school and class, and so she would therefore gain a greater sense of belonging.

In addition, Ms. Moyer added to Christina's sense of significance by assigning her the rather impressive title of homework monitor—which I believe is just one heartbeat away from homework czar. In very little time, Christina discovered that shouting out answers, although providing a false sense of significance and belonging, was not necessary, and the misbehavior stopped.

In summary, Christina's misbehavior was a textbook example of how her rationale (*Do whatever it takes to feel secure, important, and to belong*) drove her to misbehave. Once she felt more secure, she no longer needed to search for illegitimate ways (misbehaving) to meet legitimate needs.

CHAPTER 5
BECOMING A DQ DIAGNOSTICIAN

Whenever you go to the doctor with an unspecified malady, the first thing the doctor does is to ask you some questions about how you feel. Obviously, the purpose for this is to try to identify either the presence or absence of various characteristics (symptoms of familiar illnesses) in order to rule out or focus on specific ones. Since most of us cannot diagnose our own sickness, the doctor relies on our ability to tune into our *feelings* (again, symptoms) in order to narrow the field of possibilities. I've found it not only highly beneficial, but instrumental, to take the same approach throughout the DQ diagnosis. Likewise, when I work directly with parents to help diagnose their child's misbehavior motivation through DQ Factor analysis, I often use a series of DQ diagnosis tests.

To this end, each of the chapters focusing on one of the four DQ Factor types (Bears, Monkeys, Porcupines, and Lambs) will feature two separate tests. The first test is the *Feelings Experienced During Unruly Periods* test (which we came to affectionately call FED-UP), and it is designed to tap into your feelings during and after your child's misbehaving episodes. Listening to, and understanding, your feelings is powerful because it speaks volumes about your child's motives for misbehaving.

The FED-UP test was designed to be given to parents before too much was discussed about their particular disciplinary situation at home or before teaching them much about DQ Factors. The reason for this is that we parents tend to jump to conclusions about our kids and their motivations prior to having all the facts. We do this for a number of reasons. Sometimes it is just a mistaken perception of why our little one is acting like Godzilla, or it can be that we simply *want* to believe what we *want* to believe. It's no secret that we moms and dads derive a major sense of success (and failure) based on our kids.

The second test in each chapter is a DQ Factor test, which poses multiple questions about your child's or teenager's behavior characteristics: moods, attitudes, and actions. The DQ Factor study concluded that a combination of these two tests produced a definitive DQ diagnosis in 93.8 percent of the cases.

How Do You Feel?

Let me bring the DQ diagnostic analogy more into focus. Whenever a parent comes to me complaining of an unspecified, general discipline problem between her and her child, the first thing I ask is, "How do you feel during and immediately after the misbehaving incident?" Just as your family physician needs to hear the physical specifics of how you feel, I need to hear the emotional specifics of how you feel. By understanding your feelings during the entire misbehaving process (acting out—discipline—hopefully, resolution), I can better diagnose your child's DQ Factor.

The first time I ask a parent how he or she feels while the child is misbehaving and throughout the discipline process (or lack thereof), I generally receive either a blank stare or a comment like, "What do you mean, how do I feel?" This is because nobody ever asks us parents how we feel. We get so caught up in what the child did that we ignore how we felt. Once we start tuning into our feelings, we have officially entered the DQ Factor diagnostic process. In each DQ chapter there is a Parent's Emotional Response Chart (PERC) to help you determine your feelings.

EVALUATING YOUR PERC READING

If you wracked your brain and simply could not find a reasonably close match between your feelings regarding the last episode of your child's misbehavior and the emotions on the PERC, don't despair. It is very common for parents to relate that they either drew a blank while trying to recollect their emotions or that they just can't match any on the chart with how they felt. This is a new way of thinking for 99 percent of parents. Rest assured, you will become highly conversant in this new language in no time.

In contrast, there is another group of parents who will instantly tap into their experienced emotions and be able to find the corresponding emotion(s) on the PERC. Just in case you were wondering, women seem to take to this exercise more readily then men at a ratio of about 65 percent to 35 percent.

A WORD ABOUT CROSSOVER EMOTIONS

Life, let alone disciplinary issues, does not normally come in tidy bundles. Especially as you begin to become more proficient at identifying your disciplinary emotions, you will find crossover emotions. It is not at all uncommon for you to feel the irritation and control associated with kids and teens who fall under the Monkey DQ Factor while also experiencing the challenge normally associated with the Bear DQ Factor. There will be crossover emotions, but after a little practice, you will find you have become quite adept at zeroing in on the predominant emotion(s).

It is also helpful to keep a journal for the specific purpose of tracking your emotions surrounding your child's misbehaviors. And lest you think I am delusional and in need of heavy medication, I am aware that you dads reading this last paragraph just collectively rolled your eyes and scoffed at the notion. In any event, here is an example of a journal entry from a parent of a twelve-year-old:

July 31, 2002

Timmy got up this morning, and during breakfast he spilled cereal and milk all over the kitchen table and floor. When I asked him to clean it up, he said he didn't have time before he had to leave for school. I told him he had to clean it up now or the ants would get all over the kitchen. He argued with me and told me that he didn't have time. We argued some more, and I told him he would be restricted to his room after school if he didn't clean it up. He agreed to clean it up before leaving for school. I went back to getting ready for work and he left for school. When I was leaving I noticed that he had not touched his mess.

I felt angry that he didn't do what I told him to do, but I felt more challenged by him because he just makes a fight out of everything. When he came home from school, I pointed out the cereal mess and told him how angry I was that he didn't do what I told him to do. He sort of scoffed at it and made light of how ridiculous it was that I was worried about ants. He also said that I clean up after Margo and Dennis, but not after him, like that meant that I didn't love him as much. It ticks me off when he minimizes my feelings.

This mom had done a good job of listing three primary feelings concerning her son's misbehaving. She noted that she felt *angry, challenged,* and *minimized.* Her journal entry helped me to understand considerably more about her child's DQ Factor and how she experienced him.

DQ Factor Pop Quiz

It would be far too easy to simply tell you what DQ Factor her son was. Just for fun and practice as you become acquainted with this new concept, which of the following DQ Factors do you think he might be?

DQ Factor	Name	Characteristics
DQ Factor #1	Bear	Strong-willed child. Will often misbehave in challenging, controlling, confrontive ways and often just for the sake of misbehaving. Often complains about the rules and how unfair they are. Outwardly despises discipline and being told what to do. Will also routinely challenge your authority in an attempt to gain the upper hand and take control.
DQ Factor #2	Monkey	Not as strong-willed, controlling, or combative as his Bear cousin. Seems to misbehave in odd and obvious ways, knowing he will get caught and get into trouble. Misbehavior is often motivated by his need for attention from you and other authority figures.
DQ Factor #3	Porcupine	Usually quiet and not nearly as *in your face* as the Bear or as obvious as the Monkey. Is passive-aggressive in that he says everything is okay, but underneath it all, he is ticked about something. If you hurt him emotionally, he will hold on to it and figure out a way to get you back. Often, getting you back means misbehaving.
DQ Factor #4	Lamb	Not at all strong-willed like the Bear or the Monkey, and not motivated by revenge like the Porcupine. Has poor self-esteem and is convinced that he is inadequate and messes up everything. A bit of a victim thinker and will commonly misbehave to get you to take over and do things for him, which reinforces his "I'm helpless" self-image.

Based on this mom's description of her emotions as being angry, challenged, and minimized, the diagnostician in me would want to take a serious look at DQ Factor #1—Bears. Certainly Timmy was controlling and challenging to his mom by not doing what she asked him to do. Mom also mentioned that she felt minimized when Timmy scoffed at her even though she was not making a joke. Laughter is a dismissive technique used by Bears to communicate their disregard for their parent's authority. Timmy's DQ Factor #1—Bear status merits serious consideration, but it is too soon to jump to a conclusion.

Turning my focus to DQ Factor #2—Monkeys, I would have to pay attention to the possibility that Timmy was misbehaving simply as a way to get attention from his mom. The fact that she works gave us pause to consider that perhaps Timmy isn't getting enough attention and that creating a mess, and then a bigger mess, through his acting-out behavior might just be a way of garnering more attention. On the other hand, Mom clearly wrote that she felt challenged. Monkeys, although a real pain in the behavior behind, stop short of challenging their parents for control. Timmy is likely not this DQ Factor.

I would also have to consider that Timmy might be a DQ Factor #3—Porcupine. It is possible that he is punishing, seeking revenge, or getting back at his mom for something. Porcupines do tend to say hurtful things to get back at parents for perceived hurts. Another factor that makes me focus on Timmy's possible Porcupine DQ status is that he made a comment about his mom's *cleaning up after the other kids*. Remember, Porcupines act out in revenge, and it is possible that one of his younger siblings had spilled something the day before and had not gotten in trouble or had even blamed Timmy. The problem I have with this diagnosis is that Porcupines tend to be more covert in their misbehaving ways. They do things in a more sneaky fashion than to blatantly stand there and argue about cleaning up the mess. I have my doubts, but I wouldn't necessarily rule out this DQ Factor just yet.

After careful consideration I would rule out DQ Factor #4—Lambs. The reason to at least consider that Timmy might be a Lamb is that his cereal spilling episode could be construed as his need to appear helpless in order to command his mom's attention. Lambs are often joined at the hip to a parent who has a need to overprovide and keep a child too dependent. The ultimate problem I have with this DQ status is that Lambs avoid angry confrontation and challenges like they avoid wolves. To challenge and confront a parent would mean they are stronger and more self-reliant. Lamb DQ Factors need to appear more helpless and at least somewhat dependent in order to hook a parent into taking care of them. If Timmy were a Lamb, he would have spilled his cereal and then taken fifteen minutes spreading it around the floor in a thinly veiled attempt to clean it up. Finally, Mom would have gotten frustrated, snatched the rag from his little Lamblike hoof, and cleaned it up for him. Timmy is not a Lamb.

Hopefully, this exercise has provided you with a window into how much you can tell about your child's DQ simply by reading (or making) one journal entry. Even though you may not have come out of this singular exercise with a firm DQ diagnosis, we narrowed the field down to two. What we know so far is that Timmy appears to be either a DQ Factor #1—Bear, or a DQ Factor #3—Porcupine. Therefore, we can begin to treat the patient based on our understanding that he is either:

(a) misbehaving out of his need to try to control his mom, which would bring more attention and thus make him feel more loved and significant, or

(b) misbehaving because his feelings are minimized and hurt over something she has (or has not) done for him, and that his actions will somehow increase his feelings of self-worth.

In subsequent journal entries, it became evident that Timmy was in fact a DQ Factor #1—Bear. His motivation for acting out was clearly to separate and individuate from his parents (part of the maturing process). Later acts of misbehavior were clearly done to challenge his parents' rules and status in an attempt to elevate himself to adult status. In case you were wondering, this translates that Timmy was getting too big for his britches and that he wasn't as mature as he had envisioned himself.

A Concluding Thought

One of the truly fascinating discoveries to evolve from my DQ study was that, with a little practice, all parents were capable of recognizing their feelings during and after their child's misbehaving episodes. Furthermore, my staff and I came to depend on the parent's expression of feelings as an equally effective diagnostic tool to discovering their child's DQ Factor. All parents really needed was the validation that their emotions were true and relevant, and that they were not inadequate for having these emotions. Once parents understood what emotions to look for and how they translated as insights into their child's motives for misbehaving, the process of diagnosing DQ Factors became valuable.

Now that you have a foundational understanding of the four DQ Factors and how reading your emotions plays a vital role in the diagnostic process, let's take a more intimate tour of the DQ zoo. I've found that the best place to start is the Bear habitat.

CHAPTER 6

DQ FACTOR #1—BEARS

(THE STRONG-WILLED CONTROLLERS IN THE ZOO)

Bears (technically known as DQ Factor #1) are the most challenging, headstrong, and obstinate inhabitants of the DQ zoo. They also tend to be my favorite sort of children and teenagers to work with. Why? Because they are tough kids. They tend to be natural leaders, confident, somewhat driven to succeed, and smart. I also like that Bears don't allow themselves to be pushed around by other kids or even adults. They are rugged individuals who will stand up for themselves, challenge those who pick on them, and even defend less tough kids.

Another reason I particularly enjoy DQ Bear types is that my wife and I actually raised one. It should be noted that when Tracy (my daughter) was young, she was not a Bear DQ type. As she reached ages six and seven, she started to develop more of these DQ characteristics. Once she hit eight years old, she was a full-blown grizzly. Therefore, I know firsthand what it is like to raise a daughter of this DQ ilk. Presently, my daughter is eighteen and off to Bear college. She has turned into a completely lovely young woman, but rest assured, she is still two parts grizzly and one part panda. Even though she has matured beautifully and softened the edges of her naturally controlling nature, in many ways she still resembles the young Bear she was growing up. I hear it in her voice when we talk about her classes or her part-time job. This is why I good-naturedly tease her by saying, "Woe to the man who marries my daughter!"

When she mentions stressors at school, I hear it through comments like, "It is silly that the professor makes us do a paper on something that we will never use in a million years!" Or, "It's ridiculous where they tell us to park to get to our dorms. I'm going to the office tomorrow and ask them why this is the rule." I just smile and give her gentle suggestions because, deep down inside I know . . . *once a Bear always a Bear.*

Bears are not weak-minded followers who get into trouble just for being in the wrong place at the wrong time. In fact, it is usually the misguided Bear who leads others into being in the wrong place at the wrong time. I present to you that, although Bears have a tougher time trying to conform throughout life, they are more interesting to parent and are often successful because of their assertiveness and individualism. It is just getting them through their cub years that turns your hair gray.

ARE YOU EXPERIENCING A BEAR IN YOUR ZOO?

Below is a primary list of feelings that parents experience most frequently throughout the misbehaving—discipline—resolution process. To get you started on how the DQ diagnostic process works, let's start with a technique called *projected visualization.*

Step 1
Close your eyes and clear your head for one minute by trying not to think about anything. Try just focusing your mind's eye on a blank wall that has been painted light blue.

Step 2
Now think back to the last significant misbehaving episode with your child and relive all the various feelings you felt when you discovered the mis-

behavior, all the way up to the time you resolved it. Relive just those feelings for one full minute.

Step 3

Now take all of those thoughts and feelings and sum them all up in one or two words that best describe your emotions at the time.

Step 4

Now search the list of emotions below to see if any of these emotions match (or come close to) the emotions you last experienced while your child was misbehaving. The highlighted section contains the words most commonly used by parents of Bears to describe their disciplinary feelings.

PERC (Parent's Emotional Response Chart)
For use in determining child's DQ Factor

DQ FACTOR #1—BEARS

Threatened

Challenged

Angry

DQ FACTOR #2—MONKEYS

Irritated

Annoyed

Controlled

DQ FACTOR #3—PORCUPINES

Hurt

Manipulated

Minimized

DQ FACTOR #4—LAMBS

Inadequate

Pity

Frustrated

As you saw from the journal exercise in chapter 5, you don't need a deep understanding of the DQ Factors to move ahead quickly. Just the process of tuning into your feelings during and after a misbehaving episode will speak volumes about what motivates your child's actions.

With that in mind, and before you get too inundated with DQ Factor knowledge, let's set the stage for discovering all about DQ Factor #1—Bears, starting with the the FED-UP test.

PARENT FEELING EVALUATION FOR DQ FACTOR #1 TEST

The FED-UP test was initially designed to diagnose DQ Factor #1—Bears by examining the feelings experienced by the Bear's parents. What we discovered was the test not only flushed the Bears out of the woods efficiently, but it also served as a great beginning diagnostic procedure in each of the other DQ Factors as well. Remember: There are no *right* or *wrong* answers, and there is no judgment attached to this tool. It is designed only to provide you with information.

FED-UP INSTRUCTIONS

There is a particular frame of mind that I routinely ask parents to employ before they take any test regarding their children or their parenting skills. That mind-set is to try, as best you can, to separate yourself from being defensive of your own parenting skills. None of us is a natural parent; you could fill volumes of books based on just the mistakes I've made with my own kids. The key to this test is to try to be as objective as you can in your answers. Likewise, don't be concerned with how you perceive the test is going for your child either. No one but you and your spouse should ever see the results from this test, so it does no good to try to make it look better. The value of this test is in determining a *true* score and not a *hopeful* one.

Read the following questions carefully. Each has been designed to correspond to any age child or teenager. Sometimes it is helpful to answer the questions while imagining that you are actually someone else, but someone who knows every intimate detail about you and your family. Answer the questions below by circling

(a) if you *strongly agree* with the statement,

(b) if you *somewhat agree* with the statement, or

(c) if you *do not agree* with the statement.

DQ FACTOR #1—BEARS FED-UP TEST
(FEELINGS EXPERIENCED DURING UNRULY PERIODS)

When my child or teenager misbehaves and I confront the behavior with discipline, I feel the following:

1. I get angry because my child knows the rules, but often chooses not to follow them.
   Circle one: (a)   (b)   (c)

2. I get angry with my child more often than I'd like.
   Circle one: (a)   (b)   (c)

3. I struggle to show him/her as much affection as I'd like because he/she is so difficult.
   Circle one: (a)   (b)   (c)

4. It's frustrating because, no matter what punishment I choose, it doesn't seem to change things for very long.
   Circle one: (a) (b) (c)

5. Whatever the punishment, it doesn't seem to bother her/him much.
   Circle one: (a) (b) (c)

6. I feel challenged at times like, Who's in charge: me or you?
   Circle one: (a) (b) (c)

7. I get angry at times because s/he just seems to ignore my instructions.
   Circle one: (a) (b) (c)

8. It's frustrating that I have to constantly repeat myself to get her/him to follow my directions.
   Circle one: (a) (b) (c)

9. I feel embarrassed when his/her teacher tells me he gets in trouble in school.
   Circle one: (a) (b) (c)

10. I don't know what to do to get her/him to follow my instructions.
    Circle one: (a) (b) (c)

11. I feel ineffective as a parent when I have to bribe him/her to do things just to avoid hassles.
    Circle one: (a) (b) (c)

12. I go crazy because I am constantly repeating myself with her/him.
    Circle one: (a) (b) (c)

13. I worry what it will be like later if s/he is this tough to deal with now.
    Circle one: (a) (b) (c)

14. I don't know why everything has to be so difficult with her/him.
    Circle one: (a) (b) (c)

15. Sometimes I feel like s/he is putting me down.
Circle one: (a)   (b)   (c)

16. I try to avoid it, but we seem to butt heads.
Circle one: (a)   (b)   (c)

17. I get frustrated because I feel like I have to coax him/her into doing things at which I should just be able to say, "Go do it."
Circle one: (a)   (b)   (c)

18. S/he doesn't give me the respect I deserve.
Circle one: (a)   (b)   (c)

19. I'm getting worn out having to deal with discipline so often.
Circle one: (a)   (b)   (c)

20. It isn't that unusual that I catch her/him lying to me.
Circle one: (a)   (b)   (c)

21. Sometimes I get so angry with my child(ren) that I could just scream.
Circle one: (a)   (b)   (c)

22. It's confusing because s/he will tell me a lie for no apparent reason.
Circle one: (a)   (b)   (c)

23. S/he seems to respect other adults more than s/he respects me.
Circle one: (a)   (b)   (c)

24. I could use some help in getting her/him under control.
Circle one: (a)   (b)   (c)

25. I wonder what is wrong with me as a parent when I hear that other parents don't have the challenges I seem to be having.
Circle one: (a)   (b)   (c)

26. I feel angry because, at times, s/he is downright disrespectful to me.
Circle one: (a)   (b)   (c)

27. I don't like the helpless feeling I get when s/he won't listen to me.
    Circle one: (a)   (b)   (c)

28. I've been in or near tears out of frustration with her/him.
    Circle one: (a)   (b)   (c)

29. Even when s/he is being punished, s/he still challenges me.
    Circle one: (a)   (b)   (c)

30. I worry that someday I won't have enough authority to make
    him/her do what I say.
    Circle one: (a)   (b)   (c)

31. I wonder if anyone other than me knows how difficult it is to
    raise this child.
    Circle one: (a)   (b)   (c)

32. I worry about the number of squabbles s/he has with other children.
    Circle one: (a)   (b)   (c)

33. I feel powerless when the time-outs I give him/her seem to have
    little or no effect.
    Circle one: (a)   (b)   (c)

34. I wonder what to do next when even putting him/her in his/her
    room doesn't seem to have much effect.
    Circle one: (a)   (b)   (c)

35. I feel like I'm out of ideas on better and different ways to get
    him/her to behave.
    Circle one: (a)   (b)   (c)

36. It seems that I constantly have to come up with increased discipline
    to get his/her attention.
    Circle one: (a)   (b)   (c)

37. I wonder why my child always wants to be in charge when friends are over.
    Circle one: (a)   (b)   (c)

38. I think it is great that my child has natural leadership skills.
    Circle one: (a)   (b)   (c)

39. S/he always seems to have to be the first in line or the first to do something.
    Circle one: (a)   (b)   (c)

40. S/he was/is always a problem to put down for a nap.
    Circle one: (a)   (b)   (c)

41. He/she is very independent and self-reliant.
    Circle one: (a)   (b)   (c)

SCORING YOUR DQ FACTOR #1—BEAR TEST

Add up the number of (a) answers and put the number here: _____

Add up the number of (b) answers and put the number here: _____

Add up the number of (c) answers and put the number here: _____

INTERPRETING YOUR DQ FACTOR #1—BEAR FED-UP TEST

Total number of questions   41

33 or more (a) answers with any combination of other answers

If your child or teenager scored high in this DQ Factor, you are very likely living with a Bear. Do be careful, however, not to leap to conclusions. High scores do not equate at all into emotional or psychological problems. They are merely a correlation to the types of discipline your child will respond to best.

Scores at this level indicate children and teenagers who are extremely assertive (more likely, aggressive) and who love to engage and challenge you for authority in the house. This child or teenager thrives on control and does everything in his or her power to have things go his or her way. When things don't go according to plan, you can expect misbehavior as a way of challenging you.

If your FED-UP test scored at this level, you should look for confirmation with an elevated score on the general DQ Factor #1—Bear test coming up shortly.

---

23 to 32 (a) answers with 10 or more (b) answers

Very aggressive Bear DQ. You may not need as many tranquilizer darts as with the case above, but you definitely have your hands full with this one. (Caution: Do not walk around the house with raw meat in your pockets.)

---

16 to 22 (a) answers with 11 to 19 (b) answers

Moderate to lower side of aggressive Bear DQ characteristics. This child or teen will tend to mature and lose some of the aggressive and challenging characteristics when good parenting skills are applied, or will become a more challenging DQ Factor if parenting skills are weak. Our team has seen cute little pandas turn into complete grizzlies in a matter of months.

As an interesting aside, we also found that many parents scored their child in this range, although they never considered him or her a particularly strong-willed child. We found this to be more common among parents who were clearly on the easygoing personality side and who did not engage their children in struggles for control.

10 to 15 (a) answers with 10 to 18 (b) answers

Moderate to mild side of the Bear DQ scale, and actually in the average zone for most children and teenagers. This is a pretty healthy score for kids and teens—they tend to be assertive and therefore less likely to be taken advantage of by other children and adults.

---

5 to 14 (a) answers with approximately 10 or fewer (b) answers

Low Bear DQ score. It doesn't appear you have a Bear. Look for your child or teenager in another part of the zoo.

Note: It is common to find several (a) answers interspersed with (b's) and (c's). Regardless of the number of (c) answers, they serve only to rule out this DQ Factor and do not have any special significance on their own.

If this particular quiz did not flush out your child's DQ Factor, rest assured . . . one of the others will.

THE ADDAMS FAMILY

Bears come in both sexes and in all shapes, sizes, and colors. They are, however, all members of the Bear fraternity. With that said, let me introduce you to a family who took part in the study. Although officially they were Family #14, we affectionately referred to them as "the Addams Family."

Wendy, age nine, was the Addams family's middle child. She had a six-year-old sister named Gina and a twelve-year-old brother named Ben. Wendy, in many ways, was the typical lost middle child. She wasn't as cute and good-natured as her younger sister, nor as athletic and funny as her brother. Wendy was extremely bright, though, and instead of allowing herself to become lost in the family shuffle, she had taken on the role as *junior mom.*

For those of you who haven't experienced the joy of having a junior mom in the home, let me give you a brief overview. Junior moms nearly always fit into DQ Factor #1—Bears. Bears are often the oldest or middle children. As I mentioned earlier, they are generally on the serious-natured side, bossy (hence the term *bossy bear*), controlling, and want to be in charge. Bears who take on the junior mom role derive their sense of importance or significance from the fact that they are in command of their younger siblings and exert their authority by imitating their moms. They seem to gravitate to a second-in-command position behind Mom as a way of avoiding getting lost (insignificant) in the family structure. Junior mom Bears are frequently discovered bossing around, scolding, and even disciplining younger siblings. They can sometimes take it to the extreme by spanking or hitting others in a misguided attempt to correct misbehavior.

In families where moms work or are away for any reason, Bears like Wendy will naturally take over in Mom's absence. In Wendy's case, we found that her Bear instincts to be in command had progressed to the stage where she continually challenged her mom for control—even when Mom was home.

Over the course of several weeks of monitoring our Addams family, and particularly the battle for control brewing between Wendy and her mom, we noticed two interesting patterns. The first challenging Bear pattern centered around weekday (before school) rituals. The second pattern came out on Saturday mornings when the kids generally were responsible for doing their chores.

Let me give you a glimpse into Wendy's weekday problematic pattern of behavior. Everyone in our Addams family seemed to get up at 7:00 A.M., except for Dad, who was up and off to work by 6:30 A.M. Both brother Ben and sister Gina would predictably sleep through their alarms or turn them off and go back to sleep. Mom, an easygoing and fun-loving type of personality, would hit the snooze button on her own alarm clock a minimum of two times before finally getting up to get the kids off to school by 8:15 A.M. Wendy, true to her Bear DQ Factor, would awaken immediately upon hearing her alarm clock, spring from bed, and begin getting ready for school. As soon as Wendy was dressed, she would go into her little sister's room and begin the ritualistic bossing. Some mornings she might yank the covers from Gina's bed and demand she get up, while other mornings she might simply turn on her lights and shout at her to get up. Gina would, in turn, scream, "You're not the boss of me!" and the battle for bedroom supremacy would be on. To be sure, mornings in the Addams family presented a number of highly entertaining tapes.

The pattern then expanded to include Mom's intervention. After a few minutes of verbal combat between Gina and the Bear, Mom would enter the room and quietly tell the girls to knock it off and get ready for school. Wendy, a master of manipulation who would make even David Copperfield green with envy, would extend her arms and shrug her shoulders and lament, "I was only trying to help by getting Gina up and dressed for school on time." Rising to the surface to take the bait, Mom would generally scold Gina for being uncooperative when her sister was just trying to help out. And *presto!* As you can see, Mom's naive support of Wendy's controlling, I'm-in-charge-here, junior mom mentality was reinforced each time this happened.

Getting back to the crime scene, once Gina was out of bed, Wendy would hover around, prodding her and giving a verbal thumbs-up or thumbs-down to what Gina wanted to wear. After she was generally convinced that Gina was getting dressed as directed, Wendy would venture downstairs to pack lunches. When we first noticed the lunch-packing routine we thought how wonderful and sweet it was that Wendy would help out her mother in such a way. As we listened more intently to the conversations surrounding the lunch-packing ordeal, though, we noticed it was not all hugs and Twinkies.

Almost on a daily basis, Ben would protest either that Wendy was packing something that he didn't want in his lunch, or that he didn't need one as he was buying lunch that day. On days when Ben wanted to buy lunch, Wendy might make a comment about how much money it costs to buy lunch and how much less expensive it is for Mom and Dad if he takes his lunch.

Wendy's controlling didn't stop at the breadboard. Wendy would dog Ben and Gina throughout the morning ritual. If one of them stopped and watched the television, Wendy would first yell at them to get moving, and then to Mom to let her know that the two were not doing what they should be doing. Finally out the door, Wendy would race to the minivan to ensure she had first rights to the front seat ("shotgun" as she called it). This is clearly the seat of preference for all Bears, although when they get older, they want to drive all the time. Wendy's front seat came with all the perks, such as control over the six-speaker stereo and DVD player. If either of her siblings protested her movie or radio station choices, Wendy would refuse to compromise. Even after her mother intervened and insisted that it was time for one of the other children to have a turn selecting a movie or a radio station, Wendy would do something to ruin the moment. Whether it was turning off the radio, singing, or whistling loud enough to ruin the others' choices, Wendy could be counted on to be difficult if she didn't get her way. And this wasn't just once in a while, this was several times each week.

At about this time, you must be wondering what Wendy's mom was doing to counteract her controlling, bossy, and Bearlike daughter. Rest assured, Mom was trying. She would scold Wendy and make her stop badgering Gina. She would even threaten Wendy with punishment if she didn't stop tattling on her siblings every time one of them did something Wendy didn't like. One morning, however, the pattern became very clear.

It happened on the way to school. Wendy was in her usual front seat while Gina and Ben were in the back of the family's new minivan. Apparently the new minivan came with a feature that the old minivan did not have—rear radio controls. Life, as Wendy had ordained it while in the minivan, was immediately over once Benjamin figured out that he could change the radio station from the back seat. This sent Wendy into fits. She demanded that her brother stop turning off her choice in music. When her demands failed, she turned off the radio, which resulted in a shouting match and a mysteriously thrown Kleenex box that left a noticeable red mark on her brother's forehead. In essence, if Wendy couldn't control the station, no one could listen. True to her Bear form, however, Wendy read the owner's manual that evening and found the buttons used to disable the backseat stereo controls. WIN!

Before we discuss Wendy's more problematic weekend Bear behavior, please understand: Wendy was not a bad or mean-spirited child at all. She was, in fact, quite sensitive, caring, and often helpful. Although her intentions were good, her actions came across otherwise. It was on one particular weekend, however, that Wendy became one! with her inner Bear.

Wendy's family lived in Southern California and near both Disneyland and Knott's Berry Farm. Although the kids had been to both parks several times, it was always a special family day. Early in the week, Wendy's parents brought up the possibility of the family's going to Disneyland that weekend. Everyone was excited about going—that is, except for Wendy. It seemed that Wendy had been to Disneyland about one month prior for a friend's birthday party, and she was not excited about returning so quickly.

"Why can't we go to Knott's this time?" she whined.

Appealing to any reasonableness she might discover in her daughter, Mom replied, "Honey, we all just decided we hadn't been to Disneyland for a long time and that it would be fun to go. I know you were at Disneyland a while back, but I'm sure we can find lots of things to do this visit that you didn't have the time to do before."

"No!" Wendy protested. "I did everything. We rode all the stupid rides. The lines are a mile long, and it was packed. Disneyland stinks!"

Entering the conversation for the first time, Wendy's father did what many parents do when trying to pacify a Bear by stating, "How can you say that about the 'happiest place on earth' [the Disneyland slogan]? I haven't been to Disneyland for a long, long time. Maybe you can show me around to the best rides since you know it better than we do."

"NO! I'm not going. I'll stay home or go to a friend's house, but I'm not going to Disneyland. Why don't we just go to Knott's? None of us has been there in a long time."

Now it was Ben's turn to chime in. "It's my turn to choose a weekend outing, and I don't want to go to Knott's. [To his parents] You both said we were going to Disneyland anyway. Why does she always get her way?"

"SHUT UP, BEN!" Wendy exclaimed. "I don't always get my way. You wouldn't want to go back to Disneyland if you had just been there, and it's not your turn to choose anyway."

Asserting more authority—and applying a fairly innovative psychological maneuver—Mom announced, "Here's what we are going to do. We'll have a little chore contest this weekend. We'll start chores at 9:00 sharp, and whichever one of you finishes first—and the chores have to be done up to standards—gets to choose which park we go to. Agreed?"

"That's not fair! I have the hardest chores of anyone!" Wendy wailed.

"You do not, you little crybaby weasel!" her brother countered. "You try mowing the lawn every weekend!"

"Why don't you just graze on the grass, you cow!" came the retort.

"That's enough out of both of you!" Wendy's father announced, clearly annoyed. "We are going to see who chooses, just like your mom said, based on who does their chores first and does them right."

Both Ben and Wendy reluctantly agreed while their parents silently lamented that their kids made it so difficult to do something so seemingly enjoyable as going on a family outing. That was the end of the discussion for the time being.

At precisely 8:00 A.M. Saturday morning, Ben's alarm sounded, which caused him to spring from bed. Dressing in a near panic, he raced downstairs for a quick breakfast and then to start his chores. Mow the grass, empty the trash, rake the leaves around the trees. *I'll clean her clock*, he must have been thinking.

At approximately 9:00 A.M., and much to the bewilderment of her parents, Wendy sauntered downstairs in her pajamas. Only half-jokingly, Wendy's mom announced, "You better get a move on if you want to beat old Benjamin. He's almost done and about ready to start on the neighbor's lawn."

"I'm not worried about it," Wendy replied coolly.

As we monitored the conversation, we half-expected one of Wendy's parents to at least inquire about what she meant by saying, "I'm not worried about it," but again, it is not at all uncommon for parents to avoid challenging Bears (even young ones) to clarify what they mean. Bears seem to condition everyone around them to tread softly.

With that, Wendy's parents announced they were taking Gina and heading out to run some errands. "We'll be back in about two hours, and whichever one of you is finished with the chores—and if they are done right—will get to choose between the house of the mouse or Knott's. Got it?"

Immediately upon their departure, Ben continued doing his chores. He worked hard and consistently without even checking to see what his little sister was doing or how she was progressing. Had he looked, he would have seen her sitting in front of the television watching her favorite Saturday morning lineup.

When Wendy's parents returned home, they found she had done very little in the way of her chores: She had half-emptied the dishwasher, half-vacuumed a few rooms, and left the dust rag and furniture polish lying on the table. In contrast, Ben had just come inside and announced he had finished his chores.

Throwing her arms in the air out of frustration, Wendy's mom whined, "Wendy, what's wrong with you?" I can't believe you are just sitting around watching TV. You know good and well you haven't finished your chores. What do you have to say for yourself, young lady?"

"Why does it even matter, Mom? Why should I bother rushing around to do my chores just so we can end up at Disneyland anyway, because everyone knows that we always go where everyone else wants to go!"

SUMMARY

Wendy had acted in a typical and predictable Bear DQ manner. Even though she may have started out begrudgingly competing for the right to choose where the family would go, she sabotaged the process when she came to the realization that she was not in charge, nor was she guaranteed of winning. In short, she was dancing to the tune her parents were playing, and she didn't like it.

If you could have tapped into Wendy's subconscious during this process, you would have heard sound bites like these: *This isn't fair! They can't make me do anything. If I don't win I'm not going anyway. Even if I win, I might not want to go.*

Here is where Wendy's parents made their biggest mistake—and this is the case whether you're dealing with a controlling and challenging Bear DQ Factor or any of the other assorted members of the DQ zoo. Instead of confronting and determining an appropriate disciplinary action for Wendy's blatant challenge of their authority, they reasoned that it wasn't worth ruining everyone's day out. They decided to all go to Disneyland and let Wendy do her chores, plus some extra chores on Sunday. They missed or simply chose to ignore the fact that Wendy had thrown down the gauntlet and challenged them to a duel—a battle of wills.

That afternoon, they loaded up the minivan and headed off to Disneyland, where you can probably guess what happened, right? If you answered that Wendy was a little angel the whole time—you can deduct one parenting point from your score. If, however, you answered that Wendy could have substituted for any of the four main characters in the *Country Bear Jamboree*, then you are right. She made life miserable for everyone. She moped, pouted, griped, complained, dragged her feet, sulked, and basically did everything this side of kicking Goofy in the shins, to ruin everyone's day.

And now, if you could have tapped into her subconscious while at Disneyland, you would have heard something like: *Maybe I didn't win, but I'm going to make sure nobody else does either. Besides, I told them this wouldn't be fun.*

How Bears Behave (Subconscious Processing)

Earlier we discussed a bit of the psychology behind *why* children of all ages misbehave. Again, in nearly every instance of misbehaving I've studied, one of four motives, or misdirected goals, can be identified that drives kids to act out. Misdirected goals are those reasons or the rationale that, inside the mind of the child, drive him to do what he perhaps knows he shouldn't do.

Why is it important to identify your child's misdirected goal? Because once you have a sense of what your child is searching for, then you can look past the misbehavior to solve the root of the behavior problem.

THE MISDIRECTED GOAL OF BEARS IS ALWAYS CONTROL

Whether you call it wanting to be in charge or just plain bossiness—BEARS CRAVE CONTROL! Let's go back to the understanding that all humans are driven to achieve a sense of significance (importance) and belonging. Although it is not true, Bears feel most significant (most important in everyone's eyes and their own) when they are in control. Therefore, when your DQ Bear child misbehaves, he is likely doing so in an attempt to gain control, thereby increasing his self-esteem. Even if he doesn't succeed in gaining control over you, the battle itself was enough to give him a sense of self-satisfaction, power, and control. At the very least, you were drawn into battle, which in his mind means he is powerful and influential—even over you. You and I know that his sense of self-importance is hollow and manipulative, but he doesn't.

WARNING! PLEASE DON'T FEED THE BEARS

Bears are highly reactive creatures. In fact, among the four DQ Factor types (Monkeys, Porcupines, Lambs, and Bears) the latter are the most reactive in that they are the quickest to react to situations going on around them. It doesn't take much to set Bears off, although there will always be a triggering event. To best understand what I mean by a *triggering event*, perhaps an analogy would help.

If you've ever worked with, or understand, the cycles of alcoholism, one of the absolutes of *falling off the wagon* (going back to drinking) is that the actual moment that the alcoholic takes the drink is not the moment he fell off the wagon. The drink was merely the recognizable symptom of some deeper experience in his recent past that weakened his resolve not to drink. Some triggering event will always start the alcoholic cycle in motion. Although most alcoholics will tell you that they were able to identify that event later, most will admit they couldn't see it at the time. Were you to analyze the *falling off the wagon* experience you would find that a few days, weeks, or months earlier, some emotionally challenging event drove the need to drink deep within the subconscious.

For example, I once worked with a recovering alcoholic who'd been sober for ten years. One day he inexplicably took a drink and thus triggered a three-month binge-drinking cycle. In therapy with alcoholics, just as in therapy with other emotional challenges, the emphasis must always be to determine the deeper-seated *triggering event* rather than to focus solely on the symptom. This particular person had been caught up in the multiple news accounts regarding priests who had abused children in the Catholic church. Although he had successfully repressed his own abuse (at the hands of an uncle), reading these accounts triggered his old emotional wounds and drove him to seek ways to bury them again.

This is true for each of the DQ Factor types in that they exist at some level constantly. Then, after a triggering event, they accelerate. It just happens to be that Bears, with their assertive and aggressive drive to control, are the easiest to spot.

Now back to Wendy and trying to find a triggering event that might explain why she was so aggressive in her attempt to control the family's outing. By systematically going through tapes from the previous two weeks, our staff found one particular day to be of interest. You'll recall that Wendy had gone to Disneyland a month earlier for a birthday party with a classmate. In fact, that was Wendy's reasoning for not wanting to go back so soon. Although she was able to make a case for that being the reason, an earlier tape revealed that the girl who invited Wendy to Disneyland had just won an election as the class president. Take a wild guess as to who she defeated in a close runoff.

The return to Disneyland held huge emotional issues for Wendy. It wasn't that she didn't enjoy the park, or even that a large part of her didn't want to go. It was that returning forced her to confront all the feelings that went along with losing something that was very important to her. Losing the presidency to her friend meant she wasn't as popular as she thought. It also meant Wendy wasn't as *in control, respected, singled-out,* or *special* as she saw herself. In essence, she was minimized, and Bears hate to be minimized. Minimization is like a thorn in the paw to Bears. It hurts, and they want it removed instantly.

Not that it mitigates what a nasty little ill-tempered Bear-cub Wendy was being leading up to and throughout the Disneyland visit, but at least now it is better understood. Remember, DQ Bear types are the strong-willed children who gain their highest sense of belonging by feeling in charge. What could be more *in charge* than being class president? Whenever Bears sense their influence or control slipping away, they begin to feel less important in their own and others' eyes. When this happens, Bears will challenge authority by misbehaving in an effort to regain control or to at least keep you or others out of control.

COMMON TRAITS AMONG BEARS

Isn't it interesting that panda bears are among the most popular stuffed animals found in toy stores? Yet, each year it seems that there are at least a couple of news stories about how one of these real-life cute and cuddly creatures tried to make a sack lunch out of a tourist. If you happen to have a DQ Bear type, there is no doubt in my mind that he or she is cute and cuddly too. My hunch is also that, more than just once in a while, you get the sense you are little more than a sack lunch for your Bear as well.

We will get to another quiz that will help you detect whether or not you have a Bear shortly, but for now, here are some of their more prominent personality traits:

- Strong-willed kids and teenagers who want things their way
- Controllers

- Prone to temper outbursts
- Quick-tempered and slow to let it go
- Want to be the leader of any group
- Want to be first in line for everything—resist being second at anything
- Passive-aggressive (compliant to your face—angry behind your back)
- Get physical with (will push and sometimes hit) children or even adults
- Angry or aggressive behavior
- Trouble getting along with anyone in authority (teachers, coaches, parents)
- Want to be in charge in social settings
- Things must go their way or problems will result
- Crave attention and adoration of others
- Argumentative and will not admit when wrong
- Get the last word in (even if under their breath)

SYNOPSIS

Expressions such as *unbearable, grin and bear it*, and *bear with me* were likely created by parent support groups who huddled together for safety and help in dealing with Bears at home. Make no mistake about it, if you have a strong-willed Bear in your zoo, then you are likely one stressed-out zookeeper.

After raising a Bear from a cub, and through studying and knowing several hundred others, it is safe to say that Bears are more of a product of a personality type (nature) than environment (nurture). By this I mean that Bears are just born Bears—and although certain family conditions will strongly exacerbate or smooth out rough Bear traits, there is nothing you can do to make a Lamb out of a Bear. Please don't confuse this statement, however, with the fact that this book is intended to not only teach you how to spot a Bear, but how to most effectively handle your Bear so as to avoid the frustrations common with this lovable yet challenging personality type.

When studying Bears in their natural habitat, it is common to find another Bear in the family. My research has concluded that in 82 percent of the DQ Bear types I've studied, either the mom or the dad is a grown-up Bear. (Note that I resisted using the *papa bear / mama bear* terms). Occasionally a Bear will come from two easygoing non-Bear parents, but in these cases, you can generally find a grandparent Bear.

When a Bear parent has a Bear child (known as cubs in the wilderness, but as mini-controllers in your home) you are assured of an *interesting* (may substitute mind-numbing, bound-to-go-bald, Prozac-required) life. As infants, Bears tend to be even more demanding of your time and attention than other babies. Although there was not enough evidence to fully come to a conclusion, some data points to newborns who went through a bout of colic being more prone to developing into DQ Bear types.

As infants, Bears tend to be tough to put down to bed or for naps. This is likely for several reasons, but the two most prominent are that they are highly active and alert children, and they recognize that they are not in control of you when they are sleeping.

Bears want to play when *they* want to play and will pitch a fit if you don't give them the attention they expect. Bear cubs are easy to spot when you have not done what they want. They are the ones crying, tossing their diapers around the crib, or smiling and giggling while pushing the baby food jar of strained peas onto the floor. The first word out of the mouths of Bear cubs is not just no . . . it is *NO!* with an exclamation point and a furrowed brow.

Developmental milestones are an important part of how child psychologists and pediatricians evaluate a child's emotional and physical progress. The more recognizable milestones have to do with walking, talking, potty training, and when baby teeth come in. Of the four DQ Factor types, Bears (DQ Factor #1) and Monkeys (DQ Factor #2) reached these milestones the earliest. Both walked, talked, and were potty trained on an average of 2.6 months earlier than their Porcupine (DQ Factor #3) and Lamb (DQ Factor #4) cousins. No data was established for when teeth came in, but I'm guessing Bears had fully extended incisors almost from birth.

When DQ Bear types reach approximately five years of age, they tend to become the *junior parent* we discussed earlier. They take on the persona of whomever appears to be in control (emphasis on the word *appears*). During these years, Bears will come off as little adults. Even their vocabulary and expressions are mature for their age.

As you are trying to fully comprehend the motivation of this DQ type, simply think of the words *winning* and *controlling*. *Winning* means they are good, significant, important, and lovable. *Controlling* means they can keep things around them in check so none of the above can change. The odd thing about some Bears is that they don't have to have complete control or to win all the time—just as long as you don't either.

TURN YOURSELF INTO A DQ DETECTOR

You may recall the name Salvador Minuchin from earlier in this book. Minuchin was the psychologist who found it beneficial to be present in the homes of his patients in order to get a firsthand view of family dynamics during troublesome times. My staff and I found listening in on taped conversations invasive enough without the prospect of moving in for a week. The tapes provided us with all the data we needed to draw notable conclusions. One such conclusion was that nearly all parents felt *similar* feelings when confronted with similar circumstances from their similar DQ type children.

For instance, a mom of a DQ Bear who was lying would describe her feelings in very similar ways as another mom of a DQ Bear who was also lying. Let me give you an example of when this became obvious to us. We were charting the significant elements from two families when we noted nearly identical conversations taking place between husband and wife after a confrontation with their teenagers. As you read these transcripts, pay particular attention to the similarities.

FAMILY #47

PARENTS

   Mom: Murial

   Dad: Walter

CHILDREN

   Trever (age 11)

   Alicia (age 9)

   Nathan (age 7)

   Samantha (age 6)

MURIAL   *"I need to talk with you about Nate [Nathan]."*

WALTER   *"What did he do this time?"*

MURIAL   *"When I dropped him off this morning, I told him to remember to bring home his homework because I wanted him to get it done before dinner tonight."*

WALTER   *"And he didn't do it?"*

MURIAL   *"Not only that, but he sat there and looked me in the eye and lied to me. He told me that his teacher didn't give them any homework. I called his teacher and found out he was lying."*

WALTER   *"So what did you do?"*

MURIAL *"I just yelled. I got so angry. It makes me feel like he has no respect for me. How he can just straight-faced look at me and lie . . . I feel like blistering his bottom and restricting him to his room for the rest of the school year. I'm so frustrated with that kid I can't see straight."*

WALTER *"Did you tell him that you caught him in a lie?"*

MURIAL *"Yes! And it didn't even seem to bother him. He just shrugs like,* big deal, *and says something about his homework is his business! I want to strangle that kid."*

FAMILY # 61

PARENTS
Mom: Suki
Dad: Kenny

CHILDREN
Daniele (age 10)
Mark (age 8)
Justin (age 6)

KENNY *"I talked to Daniele this afternoon about her school problems and not turning in her homework."*

SUKI *"Thank you. Does she understand that Mrs. Atkins is going to start calling us whenever she doesn't turn in an assignment?"*

KENNY *"Well . . . I told her basically that, but I came away from the talk completely and totally frustrated. I mean, she just looks right through me like she doesn't care what I'm saying. I started to get really angry because she just shrugs her shoulders as if to tell me that her homework is her business. I started to get so angry and frustrated that I just wanted to strangle her."*

The similarities were remarkable and caused us to begin charting the emotionally charged conversations parents would have concerning their child's misbehavior. We paid particular attention to the words parents would use to describe how their child *made them feel* following an episode. As with each of the DQ Factor types, *parents* of Bears expressed very similar emotions during their efforts to corral the challenging and controlling behavior of their cubs. The test below was derived from the list of feelings and emotions commonly observed in parents of Bears.

A Note to Moms and Dads

If you read through and could relate to the descriptive terms above, then the chances are you are dealing with a DQ Factor Bear in your home. The following test should help to clarify if this is the case.

ARE YOU LIVING WITH A BEAR?

Now it is time to verify if you are, in fact, living with a Bear. The questions below comprise a critical mass of questions that should provide a clear-cut indication of your child's DQ Factor #1—Bear status.

As you did with the previous test, try your best to separate yourself from any emotional investment in the answers or outcome. You can best do this by imagining you are an outsider—but one who knows your child inside and out—and you have been asked to evaluate him or her.

Read the following questions carefully. Each has been designed to correspond to any age child or teenager. Answer the questions below by circling

(a) if you *strongly agree* with the statement,

(b) if you *somewhat agree* with the statement, or

(c) if you *do not agree* with the statement.

DQ FACTOR #1—BEAR TEST

1. S/he just seems to thrive on excitement and even some chaos.
   Circle one: (a)   (b)   (c)

2. If there isn't enough excitement going on, s/he will create some.
   Circle one: (a)   (b)   (c)

3. If s/he knows someone is doing the wrong thing, s/he is likely to point it out.
   Circle one: (a)   (b)   (c)

4. S/he wants to be the one in charge of setting the rules.
   Circle one: (a)   (b)   (c)

5. S/he seems so grown-up at times that I forget s/he is only that age.
   Circle one: (a)   (b)   (c)

6. If s/he were playing Monopoly or some other board game, s/he would want to be the banker or in charge of the property.
   Circle one: (a)   (b)   (c)

7. If s/he is playing with other kids and something doesn't go her/his way, you can count on trouble.
   Circle one: (a)   (b)   (c)

8. S/he is mature for his/her age.
   Circle one: (a)   (b)   (c)

9. He/she walked earlier than most children start walking.
   Circle one: (a)   (b)   (c)

10. He/she talked earlier than most children start talking.
    Circle one: (a)   (b)   (c)

11. S/he was/is more difficult to potty train than most children.
    Circle one: (a)   (b)   (c)

12. I would have to say my child is rather bossy.
    Circle one: (a)   (b)   (c)

---

13. When my child does something wrong, it is very difficult to get him/her to admit it.
    Circle one: (a)   (b)   (c)

---

14. I seldom hear my child praise others for their accomplishments.
    Circle one: (a)   (b)   (c)

---

15. When it comes to choosing places to go, my son/daughter wants to choose.
    Circle one: (a)   (b)   (c)

---

16. When it comes to dinner out, if we don't go where he/she wants to go, I'm sure to hear at least some grumbling about the choice.
    Circle one: (a)   (b)   (c)

---

17. S/he seems to be the leader or the *strong personality* among his/her peers.
    Circle one: (a)   (b)   (c)

---

18. He/she is very opinionated about likes and dislikes.
    Circle one: (a)   (b)   (c)

---

19. S/he gets along best with teachers who are easygoing.
    Circle one: (a)   (b)   (c)

---

20. S/he has had problems in the past with teachers who are more firm and by-the-book types.
    Circle one: (a)   (b)   (c)

---

21. In sports, he/she is more apt to want to be a captain or play a position where he/she can be the center of attention, such as pitcher or quarterback.
    Circle one: (a)   (b)   (c)

---

22. S/he is much more of a leader than a follower.
    Circle one: (a)   (b)   (c)

---

23. In anything competitive, he/she wants to win.
    Circle one: (a)   (b)   (c)

24. In a group of friends, he/she wants to be the center of attention or at least in charge.
    Circle one: (a)   (b)   (c)

25. Most people who know my child would agree that he/she is stubborn.
    Circle one: (a)   (b)   (c)

26. My child is not the type to be led astray into drugs or alcohol.
    Circle one: (a)   (b)   (c)

27. It would surprise me if my child/teenager were to get into trouble with the law in the future by hanging around others who were of unsavory character.
    Circle one: (a)   (b)   (c)

28. If someone gets angry with my child/teen, he/she will give it right back.
    Circle one: (a)   (b)   (c)

29. When I have to discipline my child, he/she acts like it is no big deal.
    Circle one: (a)   (b)   (c)

30. I don't know if I would use the term *tattletale*, but he/she is the first one to come and tell me when one of the other kids gets into trouble.
    Circle one: (a)   (b)   (c)

31. More often than not, I have to resort to threats just to get the chores done.
    Circle one: (a)   (b)   (c)

32. Even though I know we should talk about it, there are times when I won't bring something up because it's going to cause problems.
    Circle one: (a)   (b)   (c)

33. When he/she wants to do well in school, he/she does exceptionally well.
Circle one: (a)   (b)   (c)

34. If he doesn't want to do well in school, he/she will not do well.
Circle one: (a)   (b)   (c)

35. It is hard to motivate him/her to do things he/she doesn't care to do.
Circle one: (a)   (b)   (c)

36. My son/daughter is often overly critical of others.
Circle one: (a)   (b)   (c)

37. It is hard to get him/her to go to bed early.
Circle one: (a)   (b)   (c)

38. When he/she was young, it was hard to get him/her to take naps (or it currently is difficult).
Circle one: (a)   (b)   (c)

39. S/he has been known to say hurtful things to other kids.
Circle one: (a)   (b)   (c)

40. It is difficult to get him/her to apologize to others when he/she has done something wrong.
Circle one: (a)   (b)   (c)

41. S/he follows the rules well—as long as the rules suit him/her.
Circle one: (a)   (b)   (c)

42. S/he doesn't like to play games with others unless he/she chooses the game.
Circle one: (a)   (b)   (c)

43. I often have to do something shocking like spank him/her in order to get his/her attention.
Circle one: (a)   (b)   (c)

44. S/he resists telling me when he/she has done something wrong.
    Circle one: (a)   (b)   (c)

45. S/he may not blatantly break the rules, but he/she certainly resists the limits and boundaries I set.
    Circle one: (a)   (b)   (c)

46. S/he will test my patience at nearly every turn.
    Circle one: (a)   (b)   (c)

47. After discipline or punishment, it takes him/her a while to make me feel like everything is all right again.
    Circle one: (a)   (b)   (c)

48. If peers yell at him/her, it is likely that he/she will yell right back.
    Circle one: (a)   (b)   (c)

49. I would definitely describe him/her as more *confrontive* than *avoidant*.
    Circle one: (a)   (b)   (c)

50. S/he is one of the more active and on-the-go kids/teens I know.
    Circle one: (a)   (b)   (c)

51. When it comes to snacks, he/she is more likely to help him/herself rather than ask for them.
    Circle one: (a)   (b)   (c)

52. S/he will question adult authority rather than just going along with it.
    Circle one: (a)   (b)   (c)

53. In situations where he/she feels like he/she is being punished for something the group did, he/she will likely protest or refuse to take the punishment.
    Circle one: (a)   (b)   (c)

54. S/he doesn't (or did not) share toys and things particularly well with other kids.
Circle one: (a)   (b)   (c)

55. It is not uncommon to hear loud or even angry protests of "That's not fair!" whenever something doesn't go his/her way.
Circle one: (a)   (b)   (c)

56. S/he prefers group activities to doing things by himself/herself.
Circle one: (a)   (b)   (c)

57. When wronged, he/she is not quick to forgive and forget.
Circle one: (a)   (b)   (c)

58. S/he doesn't adapt particularly well to major changes in schedule or routine.
Circle one: (a)   (b)   (c)

59. S/he was (or is) somewhat prone to outbursts of anger
Circle one: (a)   (b)   (c)

60. Whenever he/she wants (or wanted) toys or candy in the supermarket, he/she isn't (wasn't) afraid to make his/her wants known.
Circle one: (a)   (b)   (c)

61. My child will stand there and argue with me toe-to-toe and expect me to back down.
Circle one: (a)   (b)   (c)

62. Sometimes I think s/he thinks s/he is in charge of the entire home.
Circle one: (a)   (b)   (c)

SCORING YOUR DQ FACTOR #1—BEAR TEST

Add up the number of (a) answers and put the number here: _____

Add up the number of (b) answers and put the number here: _____

Add up the number of (c) answers and put the number here: _____

INTERPRETING YOUR CHILD'S/TEENAGER'S DQ #1 TEST

Total number of questions   62

50 or more (a) answers

As previously stated, it is important to keep these scores in perspective. If your child or teenager scored high in this DQ Factor (or others), be careful not to leap to conclusions. High scores do not translate into emotional or psychological problems, nor are they an indicator of intelligence. They are merely a correlation of the type of discipline your child will respond to best. If your child or teenager scored at this level, he or she is, almost beyond a doubt, an aggressive and strong-willed Bear DQ Factor.

Don't get me wrong: After raising my own grizzly, I have a great appreciation for these kids. They are tough, verbal, opinionated, and very interesting to spend time with. If given the choice between raising a grizzly or a child who has the personality of a sea sponge, I'd take the Bear every day. On the lighter side, there may be some federal funding available when you decide to turn his bedroom into a Bear habitat.

As an aside, children and teenagers who scored above 50 also ranked in the top 5 percent in *spatial intelligence*. This is the brain's ability to visualize and think in abstract terms.

---

38 to 49 (a) answers with 20 or more (b) answers

High to moderately high Bear DQ Factor. This child is definitely assertive and strong-willed. He or she hates to lose and loves to be the one in charge when there are other kids (and sometimes adults) around.

This is the child who wants the final say on everything ranging from where the family is going for dinner to why you should give him more of an allowance.

Although he or she may not be as outwardly aggressive as the Bear at the next level up, there is no question about this elevated score—you have a Bear.

As an interesting aside, kids and teenagers who scored in the 33 to 47 range in this DQ Factor scored in the upper 10 percent of IQ.

24 to 48 (a) answers with approximately 20 or more (b) answers

This represents a moderate level temperament for a Bear DQ Factor and indicates a moderately strong-willed child. This is considered a borderline score that could swing either way. Children who score in this range are also likely to have moderate range scores in DQ Factor #2—Monkeys and moderate range scores for DQ Factor #3—Porcupines.

Regardless, we found this range to be a healthy combination of DQ Factor traits for well-balanced children. Curiously enough, children at this level scored high in creative aspects of IQ testing such as storytelling and picture drawing.

14 to 24 (a) answers with 15 or fewer (b) answers

Low on the Bear DQ Factor scale and likely only a teddy bear if a bear at all. Again, like the answer key above, do not be surprised to find that your child scores in the moderate to high range in DQ Factor #2—Monkeys in concert with this level of score.

As far as IQ measurement, these children and teenagers tested slightly above average, but were off the charts (high) in verbal intelligence.

Any other combination with fewer than 8 (a) answers and 15 or fewer (b) answers

Look elsewhere because your zoo does not have a Bear. You will likely identify your child's or teen's DQ Factor in a subsequent chapter.

Children who scored in this range were in the average group for basic intelligence but scored extremely high (upper 10 percent) in kinesthetic intelligence. That meant that they were very good with their hands, were very well coordinated, and particularly athletic.

Note: Regardless of the number of (c) answers, they serve only to rule out this DQ Factor and do not have any special significance on their own.

GENERAL ADVICE FOR PARENTS OF BEARS

In the months that followed our DQ Factor identification testing, we turned our attention to the broader task of determining what types of limits, boundaries, and disciplinary measures worked most effectively with specific DQ Factors. At first the task seemed daunting because there are so many forms of discipline. Should a parent of a Bear DQ Factor bypass warnings and go straight to other discipline? Is discipline even effective with this DQ Factor, and if so, which? To be sure, there is a discipline escalation continuum ranging from a stern look on one end to grounding in the middle to spanking on the other end.

To fully flush out recommended specific disciplines corresponding to specific DQ Factors, my team and I spent more than nine thousand hours poring over test results followed by specific case studies. As you continue to identify your children's DQ Factors, please keep in mind that when you read recommendations pertaining to types of discipline to consider and types to avoid, they have been tested repeatedly. There is, however, an important distinction between *clinical trials* and *home practice*. You, as the parent, must be the final arbiter as to the type and degree of discipline you choose under specific circumstances. Every child and parent is unique. Therefore, use these discipline prescriptions as a template for consideration and then make your best-informed decision.

One of the more frustrating things about life is that nothing happens as quickly as we want it to. That is especially true when it comes to influencing change with our kids—especially if they happen to be stubborn Bears. Rest assured, however, all Bear DQ problems can be addressed and subsequently solved through effective discipline and communication techniques.

The best place to start is to take a glimpse into the most common ways we parents fall into our Bear's trap. If your child's goal is *control*, you likely feel your authority is being challenged, which causes you to react with something resembling a battle of wills! When you tell this child to do as you instructed, she will often tell you she won't, or she'll passively ignore you. If you insist on winning by imposing punishment, she may give in temporarily, but doing so will build resentment. Even though you think you may have won, this battle is far from over.

No doubt you've heard the saying that the acorn doesn't fall far from the tree. As it applies to DQ Factor Bears, it is especially true. In nearly 73 percent of the families we studied, a Bear child or teen had either a mom or a dad (rarely both) who was also Bearlike. In adults, this DQ Factor takes on more of a controlling, dominant, strongly confident, and often inflexible parenting style. It doesn't take a Mensa candidate to figure out what happens when both Bear parent and Bear cub believe they have to win all the time.

As the grownup, it is your responsibility to change the atmosphere. Learning to compromise and work toward mutual respect, cooperation, and shared decision making will create nearly immediate change in your Bear's attitude, especially in the area of cooperation.

THE DQ UNIVERSAL ANTIDOTE

Each DQ Factor chapter will feature recommended (or prescribed) treatments. These prescriptions represent the most effective discipline and boundary techniques we observed and tested during the DQ study. There was, however, one master Rx that we found to be universally effective with each DQ Factor. The technical term for this universal antidote is called *influencing change*.

One of the most motivating, empowering, and profound messages you can take away from this book is to become a genius *influencer*. This is true irrespective of your child's DQ Factor, but especially true with Bears and Porcupines, as they tend to bristle more at challenges due to their more assertive and aggressive natures.

To grasp the concept of influencing change, think of the influencing (psychology) that goes on around you each day. We are *influenced* to buy products based on how the commercials make us *feel*. We are *influenced* to vote for a political candidate based on how we *feel* about her. We also directly *influence* the behavior in others dozens of times each day. For instance, if I had a disagreement with my wife and send flowers to her before I come home, I'm doing so for many reasons. One such reason is to *influence change* so that when I get home, I will find a warmer reception. In this analogy, how effective do you think it would be for me to try to force her to give me a warmer reception by calling home throughout the day to let her know how wrong she has been? One of my goals is to teach you to influence change in your child's behavior based on positive moves instead of threats.

Influencing behavior is best accomplished in an indirect, subtle, or intangible way. If you are a strong-willed parent and you have identified that your child is as well, then perhaps your biggest mistake would be to square off in a *mano-a-mano* grudge match to attempt to *make* your Bear change. This is a recipe for disaster, as it leads to an escalation of arms (aggressive and angry feelings and actions) on both of your parts. Or, if it doesn't turn in that direction, it will drive an emotional wedge between you and your child.

When you focus on influencing change in your child, regardless of his or her DQ Factor, you are talking about psychology at its best. Since the concept of influencing change in your child's behavior may be new to you, let me give you some examples of how this might look in your world.

CHALLENGING WAY
Angrily making assumptions that your child is responsible for something that happened before knowing the facts

INFLUENCING CHANGE
Asking questions in a neutral tone to gather facts before jumping to conclusions

---

CHALLENGING WAY
Reacting emotionally out of anger to a perceived challenge to your authority

INFLUENCING CHANGE
Responding intellectually to his challenge by refusing to get hooked into a battle of wills

---

CHALLENGING WAY
Making demands

INFLUENCING CHANGE
Making requests

CHALLENGING WAY
There is one way to do things, and that way is MY WAY!

INFLUENCING CHANGE

There are many ways to accomplish the same goal—explore them and ask which one your child or teen feels most comfortable with

CHALLENGING WAY

Telling your child what YOU think and what HE should think

INFLUENCING CHANGE

Sharing your views and asking his thoughts and opinions

CHALLENGING WAY

Telling him what to do

INFLUENCING CHANGE

Offering choices

CHALLENGING WAY

Giving ultimatums

INFLUENCING CHANGE

Asking for cooperation and compliance

CHALLENGING WAY

Going face to face to make your point while you have a good head of steam built up

INFLUENCING CHANGE

Refusing to *react* to the challenge by taking a time-out, collecting your thoughts, and responding to the situation when you are more in control of your emotions

CHALLENGING WAY

Never withdrawing from an argument or challenge to your authority

INFLUENCING CHANGE

Discussing how upsetting a battle of wills feels and suggesting taking a time-out and then readdressing it when cooler heads can prevail

---

CHALLENGING WAY

Demanding that your spouse support you in all disagreements with the kids

INFLUENCING CHANGE

Asking for your spouse's support

A CONCLUDING INFLUENTIAL THOUGHT FOR BEAR PARENTS

Remember, the challenging and confrontive nature of your mini-Bear is really just a mask for his insecurity. The more insecure he is about himself or his status among his peers, in your eyes and his own—the more he will challenge you. When you challenge Bears back, they are actually getting what they want from you. Just the fact that you engaged him in a battle of wills makes him feel more significant. In other words, he got what he wanted by hooking you into a challenge, therefore he must be fairly powerful. If, on the other hand, you learn to *influence* through thoughtful response rather than to *react*, you are disarming your Bear while teaching him how to relate to authority in an appropriate manner.

THE DQ RX FOR BEARS

As previously stated, there is a lengthy continuum of disciplinary techniques available to parents when their child has broken a rule or trounced a boundary and is in need of a measure of correction. One of the primary objectives of this study was to focus on and identify both the ineffective and effective disciplinary techniques used to correct the specific DQ Factors. My team and I found it remarkable that the majority of parents repeatedly utilized nearly identical methods of discipline—even when that discipline proved to be ineffective. This proved the theory that, when it comes to discipline, we parents have relatively few new and innovative ideas.

The list below comprises the most frequent disciplinary methods used by all parents, irrespective of their child's DQ Factor. The list is separated by type of discipline and effectiveness. In this situation, effectiveness refers to both an objective and subjective percentage we assigned to each discipline type as we witnessed its implementation and overall success rate in creating behavioral changes among DQ Factor Bears.

Type of Discipline with DQ Factor #1—Bears	Effectiveness
AGGRESSIVE SPANKING	8 PERCENT

This term refers to any spanking technique that ranged from taking the child's pants down to spank him with an open palm, to utilizing a spanking instrument such as a wooden spoon, wooden hanger, paddle, etc.

Note: There were no abuse issues throughout the study. Societal standards still view spanking with objects that do not leave permanent marks to be acceptable. For the record, I am not opposed to spanking, but I am opposed to using any instrument (spoons, hangers, belts, etc.) to spank children. Utilizing these items can clearly inflict excessive and unintentional injury.

SIMPLE SWATTING	23 PERCENT

This term refers to a spanking technique that would be called a simple swat (or series of swats) to the child's behind, delivered by an open hand to the outside of the pants and/or underwear.

IGNORING   81 PERCENT

As you can see, ignoring was one of the most effective methods of dealing with DQ Factor Bears. Ignoring is the predesigned practice of not letting your child's attention-seeking misbehavior get to you.

For instance, when your child acts out in a clear effort to challenge you, the rule of ignoring simply states to continue doing what you are doing. Don't let your child see that he has gotten to you or he will continue to pull the strings and you will continue to do your little puppet dance.

Ignoring also requires you to be in control of your nonverbal signals (facial expressions, sighs, groans, etc.). I liken this approach to being confronted by a strange dog (no offense intended with the analogy) who snarls at you. If you show signs of fear or you run, you are meat. Likewise, sending your DQ Factor Bear verbal and nonverbal signals that he is getting to you during the ignoring process will immediately nullify its desired effects. More on ignoring later.

VERBAL REPRIMANDS   23 PERCENT

This form of discipline did not work effectively with Bears for a number of reasons. Primarily though, it was because the verbal reprimand accomplished their objective of getting attention. On top of that, the reprimand (put-down) triggered more insecurities, which caused this DQ Factor to act out even more to garner attention.

TIME-OUTS 73 PERCENT

Bear DQ Factor types are highly social creatures. Therefore, removing a Bear from outside stimuli through time-outs in his room proved highly effective. The reason it works so well is that he is seeking attention through misbehavior. When his attention-seeking actions result in isolation (the opposite of attention), he is forced to deal with his needs in more appropriate ways.

RESTRICTIONS 54 PERCENT

Restrictions in this decade seem to be the grown-up big brother of time-outs. Whereas a time-out was generally seen as less than a half-hour in the child's room, we found that restrictions averaged 24 hours. We also found that restrictions commonly started out as longer terms (two to six hours in the room), but were commuted (reduced) as the talented Bear pleaded his case before the judge.

Parents (especially parents of this DQ Factor) who set longer restriction periods of three to five days—and then followed through—were much more apt to gain compliance later. These were not restrictions to a room but to the house, or restrictions on television or other enjoyed activities.

We noted that Bears detested, but later became much more compliant with, parental rules when they experienced restrictions of 24 to 48 hours of at least partial confinement to their rooms. That translated into coming out for meals, school, or after-school sporting activities and the like. When they were home, they were back in their rooms until bedtime.

We also found that parents who restricted their kids to their rooms for periods of three to seven days experienced more acting-out behaviors both during and after the punishment. The rationale behind this seemed to be that the alienation (separation) from the family created too many insecurities, which then caused the child to act out to garner more attention.

TAKING AWAY PRIVILEGES   69 PERCENT

Taking away privileges such as TV, stereo, or bike proved to be an effective tool for parents of Bears. Because this DQ Factor relies so heavily on outside stimuli to stay busy, removing important things following a behavior problem served as a reminder for future violations.

The second reason that taking away privileges was as effective as it was stemmed from its connection to natural consequences. For example, if your two children were fighting over who gets control over the TV remote (clearly, two boys), then calmly unplugging the TV would serve as both a removal of a privilege as well as a natural consequence. Keep in mind that the key is to do all of this in a calm, matter-of-fact manner.

BELITTLING   2 PERCENT (OR LESS)

Completely ineffective! If you set out to destroy your child's emotional security and sense of well-being (especially among DQ Factor Bears), belittling would definitely be your first choice. Perhaps only second to intimidating techniques, this form of discipline is destined to lead to increased immediate conduct problems, as well as more serious future conflicts.

THREATS   17 PERCENT

Making a threat is something parents do when they know they are weak when it comes to consequences.

We discovered that parents of DQ Factor Bears often found themselves feeling trapped and at their wit's end. These feelings caused them to resort to making threats in an attempt to get their kids to comply and behave.

We found another common thread running through these parents as well. They tended to make threats and then neglect to enforce the consequences. This scenario caused the children to disregard not only future threats, but legitimate requests. Keep in mind that a boundary is only a request if it does not have a communicated, understood, and fully anticipated potential for consequences.

THE DQ RX

In addition to the insights gained by examining the aforementioned typical forms of discipline used in conjunction with DQ Factor Bears, our research also produced some other, less common boundary and discipline techniques. We found the following Rx actions and ideas to be powerful in neutralizing the acting-out qualities and characteristics of Bears.

Rx #1

ACKNOWLEDGE, RECOGNIZE, AND OWN YOUR PART

At the risk of sounding like a twelve-step knockoff, the first step is always in admitting and understanding that there is a problem in the way you and your child communicate and relate. It is also important to admit that the discipline techniques you have employed simply have not been effective, and that things are not looking up.

Simply by reading this book, you have taken a great first step in understanding the new world of DQ and how your discipline responses can impact your child's future. After you have taken this bold step of identifying your child's DQ Factor and how it relates (or doesn't relate) with your own personality, you are then ready to move forward.

A good first step is to lovingly and gently call your child's attention to the fact that the two of you (own your part) have been struggling for control. Let your DQ Factor Bear know that, as much as you value her opinion and feelings, and love and respect her and her assertiveness (and want her to continue to stand up for herself), you are the parent in the family and you are responsible for making the decisions in the family. Often, just by putting words to, and sharing these thoughts with, a DQ Factor Bear, you have set the tone for a more cooperative relationship where you are owning your part in getting along.

Rx #2

IGNORING 101 OR DON'T LET YOUR BEAR FISH YOU

Bears (both the four-legged and DQ varieties) are champion fishers. Do you ever feel like you are a salmon in one of those wildlife documentary shows? You know the ones where the fish swims upstream and then, in midjump, some grizzly makes it his lunch. Well, guess who's coming to lunch? Because if you live with a Bear, more often than not, you end up being lunch.

The principle of ignoring or *letting the bait float by* simply means you and your child have a lot of history. Whether it is a battle of wills or his constant wearing you down to get his way, it all starts with an out-of-hand situation (the bait). Learn to identify the bait in your relationship. Bait can be seen as well as heard. You may see it in a disrespectful expression or downright dirty look. Or it may be heard in backtalking or a rebellious statement like, "I'm not going to do my chores right now." In any case, letting the reactive emotions pass means not rising to take the bait. When things have cooled down, you can respond.

Another effective ignoring technique involves calling attention to your child's misbehavior, but ignoring the disciplinary part of it. For instance, let's say that when your Bear doesn't get his way, he likes to stomp his feet, fold his arms, and protest your total lack of fairness. The real you would like to grab him by his little Bear arm, order him to knock it off, and drag him to his room for the next sixteen years. The ignoring approach would be to calmly look him in the eye (use your steely-eyed look if you've got one) and say, "I won't talk with you or even consider your point of view when you act that way. I am going to be in here taking care of some things. When you feel like you can talk to me with respect, then I'll be happy to listen. Until then, I want you to go to your room and consider what I've said."

This approach disarms Bears and forces them to contain their challenging ways.

Rx #3
INFLUENCE CHANGE BY NOT CHALLENGING YOUR BEAR

The absolute worst approach a parent can take while setting boundaries and disciplining a Bear DQ Factor is to challenge him to a battle of wills. Bears will naturally challenge you right back. Parents of Bears should become as familiar as they can with the subtle art of influencing their child to do the right thing because it is *right* versus because they said so. Keep referring to the *Challenging Way/Influencing Change* section provided earlier. The sooner you learn the language of influencing change through mutual problem solving, the sooner you will extricate yourself from Bear battles. There is more honor in sidestepping conflicts than there is in going head to head and winning.

Of the four DQ Factors, Bears are the fastest to respond to influencing change versus challenging ways, but all DQ types will do better with this approach.

Rx #4

SWITCH TO SMART-BOMB DISCIPLINE FOR YOUR BEAR

More than any other DQ Factor, Bears resent and resist being blamed, attacked, or anything that even remotely looks like they are being picked on.

With this in mind, here's a rather graphic analogy, but it works. Think back to the latest CNN war footage from Iraq. Flash back to the images of the laser-guided smart bombs hitting their targets with precision. With smart bombs, the target is narrow and the accompanying message sent by hitting it is loud and clear. There is little collateral damage because the bomb is designed to take out just the target. That is the way discipline should be.

Let me give you an example. I don't have any personal problem with recommending an occasional spanking when warranted. The most appropriate reason to spank a child is not because he did something wrong, but because he blatantly challenged your authority by looking right at you and doing what you told him not to do. Such assaults on your authority demand immediate and appropriate corrective action.

The problem comes when the child does something directly in conflict with what you have told him not to do. Let's say your seven-year-old asks if he can have cookies a half-hour before dinner. You oblige with the compulsory

"No, you'll spoil your dinner" line. Upon returning to the kitchen several minutes later, you see cookie crumbs all over the counter, and he has chocolate on his mouth. You ask him if he took the cookies, and he looks you square in the eye and swears he couldn't identify an Oreo if you put a lineup in front of him. Clearly, the little bugger is lying.

It is completely understandable that this event should anger and upset you. It is, however, your REACTION that will either classify this as a *smart-bomb* discipline or a *carpet-bombing* mission. Carpet-bombing means you lump all the anger and frustration at all the challenges you have endured over the past month or two into one episode. Carpet-bombing discipline means you launch into a monologue about how bad he is and how he *always* lies to you, how he *never* respects what you say, how he *isn't* compliant like his sister. Then, after the ground assault on his self-esteem is over, you launch a carpet-bombing discipline air strike by spanking him and restricting him for lying.

Don't confuse what I am advising to mean I don't believe lying warrants discipline, because it does. The problem is that spanking your child, or restricting him after you have mass-assaulted his self-esteem by using blanket terms like *always* and *never*, is just bad. Then you followed that with a harsh comparison to another person who is much *nicer, better,* and more *compliant*. You can see how damaging that can be. If you are the parent of a Bear DQ, this will further drive the challenging behaviors in the future.

If you were to employ smart-bomb discipline technology in this situation, it would look very different. First and foremost, you would never (ever) lump in sins of the past by using words like *always* and *never*. Instead, you painstakingly use terms to isolate the infraction, such as, "This is not like you. I see you as such an honest little guy that it surprises me that you would take a cookie after I said you could not. But the thing that hurts my feelings is that you would look me in the eye and lie to me about taking it. I might expect that of someone else, but not from someone as honest as I know you to be."

Yes, this is a psychologically manipulative way of dealing with an infraction, but it produces internal guilt in that the Bear let you and himself down by doing what he was told not to do, and he doubly let you both down by lying about it. Lock into your mind that it is your ability to transition him from an externally driven person ("Do what I tell you to do or you will get in trouble") into an internally driven person ("Do the right thing because it is right to do the right thing"). It is the Bear's sense of *guilt, embarrassment,* and mild *shame* that will ultimately drive this transition.

From here you need to let the discipline fit the crime. Instead of the carpet-bombing tactic of restriction and spanking, you might consider something I tried with my seven-year-old daughter (the Bear) over a similar situation. Seeking her input on what would be an appropriate punishment, we arrived on a cookie-less lifestyle for one week. Then, the punishment for lying to me was for her to say into a tape recorder one minute's worth of why she thought she lied to me about eating the cookies and what it felt like after being caught. Trust me when I say this smart-bomb discipline strategy is much more effective at influencing change than its carpet-bomb discipline counterpart. Besides, the tape can be used as a short-term and long-term reminder right up to her wedding day! Maybe even with the grandkids!

Rx #5
Bears Resist Arbitrary Boundaries

Any time you employ Gestapo tactics—fear, manipulation, intimidation, or that "It's my way or the highway" attitude—in an attempt to keep your Bear under control, you may win the temporary battle of the wills, but rest assured—you will lose the war.

Whenever you demand compliance from your Bear by setting rigid and arbitrary limits—you will eventually drive him away. It is far more preferable to develop a boundary-setting style that asks for compliance rather than demanding it.

Finally, if you are the type of parent who finds it difficult to admit when you are wrong or when someone else has a better idea, let your Bear win once in a while—especially when he or she is correct.

Rx #6
BEARS NEED QUANTITY TIME

There is a misnomer that quality time is all that counts when it comes to our kids. The truth is that the right mix is something more like 50/50 between quality time and quantity time. Too many parents make the mistake of saying, "I don't have much free time, so when I do, I sit down with my kid and we have some quality time."

Look, I've been a dad for eighteen years, and a shrink for a bunch more, and I'm not sure I can define *quality time*. Sometimes just hanging out with your kid is quality time. I actually think waiting for the quality-time bell to go off before you hang out with your kid is very destructive. Find out what your kid likes to do and go do it (even if it means playing Barbie with her), because that is quality time.

As it applies to your Bear and the issue of quantity versus quality of time, bear in mind (I knew I could get that in somewhere) that your child's self-esteem is directly tied to how much one-on-one (quality and quantity) time you spend together. When his self-esteem diminishes, a Bear's natural reaction is to challenge you for control in order to feel more significant, and therefore, esteemed.

Rx #7

Employ Natural Consequences Whenever Possible

A moment ago you read my example of having my daughter go without Oreos (cruel and unusual punishment, and long since forbidden by the Geneva convention) for her indiscretion. Whenever possible you want to employ *natural consequences* for your child's misbehavior. Natural consequences can be difficult at first to figure out. This is because we are so well versed at handing out disconnected consequences.

Let me give you an example. A close friend of mine has a teenage son who disregards his father's wish to not walk around the house in his bare feet after he has been barefoot outside playing with the dogs. It is true that you could say that my buddy is a bit of a *germophobe*, but still, it is his house and his rules. He has gotten very angry and tried all the usual discipline methods to get his son to comply, but nothing has worked. I suggested he try going the opposite way and insert a natural consequence. My suggestion included explaining to his son why he had issues with him walking around spreading germs. Then I had him ask his son if he could comply with his wishes even though he might think it is silly. This is an effective technique in that it tells your child that you are owning that the request might seem a little weird to him, but asks for compliance anyway. His son agreed to do better.

Later that day, my friend found his teenage son walking around barefoot after playing outside. Undoubtedly the horrible flesh-eating virus outbreak was already well on its way, but he decided to apply our previously discussed discipline strategy anyway. The plan was for him to resist getting angry or sarcastic at all costs. He was to calmly bring in a bucket (filled with whatever it is that germophobes like to use on their floors) and a mop and very calmly ask his son if he would "Do me a big favor." I've always liked that line as an entree into a natural consequence.

My friend proceeded to ask his son if he would mind mopping the floor so that when the little kids got home, they wouldn't crawl around the floor and pick up any germs that had been tracked in.

Because he approached his son without anger or blame—coupled with asking if he could do him a favor—the son agreed. Then it was time to apply the final twist of the disciplinary knife. My friend, just as he was coached, asked for one more favor. "Son, I realize that it just isn't as much fun running around with the dogs in the backyard with shoes on, and perhaps it was unfair of me to insist. So what I've done is to move a bucket, a mop, and a bottle of germicide to the pantry. Would you do me a favor and, right after you run around out there and come in, would you grab the mop and give the floor a good scrubbing? That way you don't have to worry about tracking in a bunch of germs that your little brothers and sister might find. Does that seem more fair to you than my constantly bugging you about putting on your shoes?"

Whether his teenager realized it or not, my friend had surgically performed a perfect natural consequence. His son had no response but to agree that it seemed more fair and that he would mop the floor after playing barefoot in the backyard.

Weird germophobe example aside, this technique works like wonders.

Rx #8

PUTTING YOUR BEAR TO WORK (THE DECK OF CHORES)

Before you run out and report me to the Society for the Prevention of Cruelty to Animals, what I am referring to is giving your misbehaving Bear extra chores to do as a discipline.

One of the techniques I found most effective with both children and teenagers in our study was an ingenious idea we called The Deck of Chores.

Using between ten and fifty blank four-by-six cards, write a different chore on one side and the card number on the reverse. Make sure you write age-appropriate chores for your child so you do not have your three-year-old changing the spark-plugs on your Oldsmobile.

When your child misbehaves and it is time to decide on his discipline, we found that a visit to The Deck of Chores was both entertaining and effective, but it did something for Bears that we had not anticipated. Because the child was the one to select a discipline chore from the deck, he could not really blame the parent for making him do something he hated to do. The choice of chores was his alone. Give it a try.

Rx #9

INVOLUNTARY DISCLOSURE

They aren't precisely what I would term disciplinary techniques, but there are several interrogation methods that I first discovered as a police officer (no bright lights, bamboo shoots, or rubber hoses) and later found most helpful with my patients as well as my kids. For some unknown reason, involuntary disclosure techniques were very effective while handling Bear DQ Factors.

I began referring to this technique as *involuntary disclosure* because it represents nonverbal cues that detect another's thoughts or emotions. The reason these cues are so helpful is that getting at the emotional truth behind actions—such as our child's misbehavior—can be guarded by the subconscious, and therefore be invisible to the individual. Or, the child may simply not want to reveal the real reason he chose to act out. Either way, involuntary disclosure will help you in learning the DQ Factor motive (control, attention, revenge, or defeatist) behind your child's misbehavior.

The interviewing techniques involve asking specific questions and then looking for subtle changes. Here are the things to look for any time you ask a sensitive question of someone and he or she either doesn't consciously know, or does not want *you* to know, the truth.

Change in facial expression

Look for the eyebrows to move up and for the mouth to adjust as though the individual is biting his lip. This is an indication that the person is uncomfortable with a question (it's hitting close to home) or he is lying.

Face flushing

Embarrassment and guilt register the same emotions in the central nervous system. If the person flushes red as though embarrassed, you are on to a sensitive area or he is lying.

Diverting eye contact

When we lie to someone, we automatically divert eye contact. This is called a *shame-based response*. Whenever you are talking to your children, look them square in the eyes. When they tell you a lie (or half-truth), they will look away momentarily, or in some cases, longer.

Involuntary shifting

Kids and teenagers will nearly always shift their weight from one foot to another or from side to side when they are uncomfortable about a question. Take note of such movements, as it means you are either on the right track with your probing questions or he is lying.

Involuntary smiling

It's amazing, but children and teenagers will involuntarily smile or laugh when you ask a question that scores a direct hit. For instance, if you were to ask your child why he carved his name into the windowsill, he will likely reply, "I don't know." If you ask him if he did it to get back at you for not letting him have that pocket knife he wanted, you are likely to see an involuntary smile or nervous laugh.

The Vegas nerve

No, this is not the mechanism that enables gamblers to place large bets. This is the technical name for the large nerve that runs vertically through the temple and down the neck. When an individual is either subconsciously covering up information or lying outright, this nerve will twitch, caused by an increase in respiration and subsequent blood pressure. You have to look carefully to spot this one, but it is a can't-miss truth detector.

SOME DQ FAQs BEFORE CONTINUING THROUGH THE ZOO

Now that you are getting familiar with how the DQ Factor diagnosis procedure works, let's stop the DQ tour for a moment to answer some common questions before moving on to the Monkey habitat.

Here is what most parents ask at this point before moving ahead:

Q: I've identified a few, or even several, DQ Bear traits in my child. His score, however, wasn't very high in the DQ Factor we just evaluated. Is it possible he might be a Bear DQ, but still score in the low range on the tests?

A: No. If your child were a Bear DQ Factor, he or she would have scored in the upper levels of the tests. It is more likely he is one of the other DQ Factors, but has some Bear characteristics.

Q: Is it a good idea for my spouse to evaluate our child using the same test so we can compare answers?

A: Yes, but a word of caution. Parents often see the same child (and his or her associated discipline issues) from a slightly different perspective. Like IQ tests, DQ Factor tests are not an exact science. There is room for interpretation, but the DQ tests overall have an 88.9 percent accuracy rate.

Q: Is it normal for a child to score in the moderate to upper range in more than one DQ Factor?

A: It is normal for kids and teens to have one elevated DQ Factor score. This is called the *dominant DQ*. At the same time, it is also common to have a secondary, or *subdominant DQ*. When it comes to Bear DQ types, a moderate score usually indicates you will find an elevated score among the remaining three DQ Factors.

Q: If a child scored moderately high on the Bear DQ Factor test, is there another DQ Factor that you have seen that often accompanies Bears?

A: Yes. In approximately 44 percent of our test cases, we saw kids and teenagers who scored moderate to high Bear DQ scores also score moderate to high in either the Monkey or Porcupine DQ Factor tests.

Q: Does it mean a child is abnormal if he scores high on one of the DQ tests?

A: Not at all. Keep in mind that the results used to measure your child's DQ Factor are based on normal misbehaviors among kids and teens. So to the contrary, when your child registered in the upper levels of any DQ Factor tests, it means he has lots of company.

Q: Should I be worried about my child if he or she scored extremely high on one of the DQ Factors?

A: At the risk of costing thousands of therapists a few therapy sessions, the answer is NO. Again, these DQ Factors were based on *normal* responses, not abnormal ones.

Q: What if a child doesn't show up as a dominant DQ on any of the DQ Factor tests? Is that possible?

A: We found only about 8 percent of the children and teenagers truly could not be identified as any dominant DQ Factor. In these cases, they had low to moderate scores in at least two of the four Factors. Kids who fit this odd pattern were often just normal kids who didn't act out in the typical way that kids do. We did, however, find that when a spouse or objective third party answered the same questions, a dominant DQ Factor often showed up.

Now that we've completed our tour of the Bear menagerie, let's pick up any stragglers and continue our tour of the DQ Zoo. Next stop—the Monkey habitat.

CHAPTER 7

DQ Factor #2—Monkeys

(The Manipulators and Attention-Getters in the Zoo)

In general our little nonprimate friends, known as DQ Factor #2—Monkeys, are often strong-willed little critters. Some monkeys are perhaps just as strong-willed as their DQ cousins the Bears; however, the main DQ difference between the two is that Monkeys are acting out to get your attention, whereas Bears act out to challenge you for control. Another difference is that our attention-seeking DQ Factor Monkeys are often more manipulative and passive-aggressive than DQ Factor Bears, who tend to be more in your face. Monkeys do enjoy an occasional challenge when it comes to undermining your authority; they just do it for the attention and not for control. Monkeys are masters at tactical manipulating.

Let me give you some further differentiations. A Bear DQ will disobey your direct order and, when challenged, will voice opposition, adamant excuses, and why you were wrong to do what you did. Monkeys, however, will shrug their little monkey shoulders and proceed with a diatribe of how you must be remembering incorrectly, or how they thought you meant something else. Monkeys can even have you believing you have gone temporarily insane and that they are right and you are wrong. They hope that the sooner you just realize that you have lost your marbles, the easier life will be for both of you.

It's easiest to understand this DQ Factor if you just keep in mind that Monkeys love and crave attention! For them, their life ambition is to attain significance by being *noticed*. They live to capture your attention and will stop at nothing to get it. They will be cute and cuddly as long as cute and cuddly works. Once they sense that C & C isn't cutting it any longer, they will shift gears to whatever it takes—including misbehaving. Once they get your attention, they feel significant, important, and therefore loved. Then, all is well in the Monkey habitat.

To sum it up, unlike their Bear DQ buddies, Monkeys will seldom come right out and challenge your authority in order to gain significance, importance, and love. They will, however, command your attention one way or another.

ARE YOU EXPERIENCING A MONKEY IN YOUR ZOO?

Below is a primary list of feelings that parents experience most frequently throughout the misbehaving—discipline—resolution process. To remind you how to get started in the diagnosis process, let's go back to the technique called *projected visualization*.

Step 1

Close your eyes and clear your head for one minute by trying not to think about anything. Try just focusing your mind's eye on a blank wall that has been painted light blue.

Step 2

Now think back to the last significant misbehaving episode with your child and relive all the various feelings you felt when you discovered the misbehavior, all the way up to the time you resolved it. Relive just those feelings for one full minute.

Step 3

Now take all of those thoughts and feelings and sum them up in one or two words that best describe your emotions at the time.

Step 4

Now search the list of emotions below to see if any of these emotions match (or come close to) the emotions you last experienced while your child was misbehaving. The highlighted section contains the words most commonly used by parents of Monkeys to describe their disciplinary feelings,

PERC (PARENT'S EMOTIONAL RESPONSE CHART)
FOR USE IN DETERMINING CHILD'S DQ FACTOR

DQ FACTOR #1—BEARS

Threatened

Challenged

Angry

DQ FACTOR #2—MONKEYS

Irritated

Annoyed

Controlled

DQ FACTOR #3—PORCUPINES

Hurt

Manipulated

Minimized

DQ FACTOR #4—LAMBS

Inadequate

Pity

Frustrated

If you found any of your answers under DQ Factor #2—Monkeys, then you have your first affirmative indication that your child or teenager may be of this DQ Factor.

Just as you used the earlier test to determine if you are living with a Bear, take a few moments to collect your thoughts and take the DQ Factor #2—Monkey FED-UP Test. As you do, continue (as you did above) to monitor your feelings in regard to your child's last misbehaving episode. Tune in particularly to how you felt during and after the disciplinary process. By paying attention to your feelings, the FED-UP Test should help you in diagnosing your child's specific DQ Factor.

PARENT FEELING EVALUATION FOR DQ FACTOR #2 TEST

The key to this test is to try to be as objective as you can in your answers. Likewise, don't be concerned with how you perceive the test is going for your child. No one but you and your spouse should ever see the results from this test, so it does no good to try to make it look better. The value of this test is in determining a *true* score and not a *hopeful* one.

FED-UP INSTRUCTIONS

Read the following questions carefully. Each has been designed to correspond to both children and teenagers. Sometimes it is helpful to answer the questions while imagining that you are actually someone else, but someone who knows every intimate detail about you and your family. Answer the questions by circling

(a) if you *strongly agree* with the statement,

(b) if you *somewhat agree* with the statement, or

(c) if you *do not agree* with the statement.

DQ Factor #2—Monkeys FED-UP Test
(Feelings Experienced During Unruly Periods)

When my child or teenager misbehaves and I confront the behavior with discipline, I feel the following:

1. If I have been busy, preoccupied, or away from my child for a while, I can almost anticipate some sort of problem.
    Circle one: (a)   (b)   (c)

2. When my child misbehaves, I get the feeling s/he is doing it more for attention than for any other reason.
    Circle one: (a)   (b)   (c)

3. I sometimes feel manipulated by my child when I ask her/him to do things and s/he acts helpless.
    Circle one: (a)   (b)   (c)

4. When my child misbehaves, I get the feeling s/he wants me to believe it was my fault that it happened.
    Circle one: (a)   (b)   (c)

5. My child is pretty good at getting me to do things that s/he is perfectly capable of doing on her/his own.
    Circle one: (a)   (b)   (c)

6. I feel manipulated at times that my child takes advantage of my easygoing or good nature.
    Circle one: (a)   (b)   (c)

7. Sometimes I feel frustrated more than anything else when s/he misbehaves.
    Circle one: (a)   (b)   (c)

8. When it comes to setting limits and boundaries, this child tests my patience to the max.
   Circle one: (a)   (b)   (c)

9. I get the sense that when I get really busy and can't spend as much time with him/her, that's when s/he will do something to get into trouble.
   Circle one: (a)   (b)   (c)

10. Sometimes I just feel like I have to get away because I have no more attention left to give.
    Circle one: (a)   (b)   (c)

11. I think I feel more guilt than I should based on how much of my attention s/he seems to need.
    Circle one: (a)   (b)   (c)

12. Among my kids (or those I know), s/he is the most demanding.
    Circle one: (a)   (b)   (c)

13. I sometimes feel as though s/he starts problems with his/her siblings (or friends) just to get my goat.
    Circle one: (a)   (b)   (c)

14. When I have to resort to disciplining him/her, I end up feeling guilty even though I've done nothing to feel guilty about.
    Circle one: (a)   (b)   (c)

15. I feel guilty because s/he says something that makes me feel like I'm not giving her/him as much attention as the others in the family get.
    Circle one: (a)   (b)   (c)

16. S/he puts me in a position that makes me nag him/her constantly about chores, schoolwork, or other obligations.
    Circle one: (a)   (b)   (c)

17. I wouldn't want him/her to hear me say this, but he/she just annoys me to tears at times.
    Circle one: (a)   (b)   (c)

18. Sometimes I feel like s/he just knows which buttons to push to get to me.
    Circle one: (a)   (b)   (c)

19. Getting him/her to do what is expected must be what the term high maintenance was invented for.
    Circle one: (a)   (b)   (c)

20. I'll tell him/her not to do something and turn around, and s/he is doing it again.
    Circle one: (a)   (b)   (c)

21. After I get mad and resort to discipline, it almost feels like s/he will punish me by avoiding me or giving me the silent treatment.
    Circle one: (a)   (b)   (c)

22. One of the most frustrating things about punishing my child is putting up with all the drama (crying, screaming, yelling, etc.) that follows.
    Circle one: (a)   (b)   (c)

23. I get the feeling that s/he doesn't even listen to me when I'm scolding her/him because I see the same behavior repeated later.
    Circle one: (a)   (b)   (c)

24. Sometimes this child makes me crazy with her/his impulsive, act-before-thinking nature.
    Circle one: (a)   (b)   (c)

25. I feel like my child needs to be the center of attention and will step all over anyone to get it.
    Circle one: (a)   (b)   (c)

26. Sometimes I feel so inadequate around her/him.
    Circle one: (a)   (b)   (c)

___

27. There are times that I feel like s/he is just so much smarter than I am.
    Circle one: (a)   (b)   (c)

___

28. S/he makes me feel like whatever punishment I hand out is just no big deal.
    Circle one: (a)   (b)   (c)

___

SCORING YOUR DQ FACTOR #2—MONKEY FED-UP TEST

Add up the number of (a) answers and put the number here: _____

Add up the number of (b) answers and put the number here: _____

Add up the number of (c) answers and put the number here: _____

INTERPRETING YOUR DQ FACTOR #2—MONKEY FED-UP TEST

Total number of questions   28

21 or more (a) answers

If your child or teenager scored high in this DQ Factor, be careful not to leap to conclusions. High scores do not translate into emotional or psychological problems. They are merely a correlation of the type of discipline your child will respond to best.

Very high on the manipulative DQ scale for Monkeys. During our study, we jokingly (easier to joke if it isn't your own child) referred to these kids as more apelike than monkeylike. Twenty or more answers in this section can also be an indication that you are dealing with a child who has many of the disciplinary needs and characteristics of DQ Factor #1—Bear.

14 to 20 (a) answers with approximately 10 (b) answers

You definitely have a Monkey in your home. Scores in this range indicate an aggressive pattern of manipulating you into paying attention. Although this child may not be as aggressive and controlling as is the case with higher scores, you are likely feeling stressed and tested to the limits. In your predawn hours of peace, you probably wonder why this child was put on earth to make you crazy. Fear not, help is on the way.

9 to 13 (a) answers with approximately 5 to 8 (b) answers

Moderate Monkey DQ Factor. Definitely not an ape. Perhaps one of those cute little ring-tailed varieties that is easy to deal with about 75 percent of the time, but the other 25 percent of the time—when he or she is feeling neglected and in need of attention—can be a real doozy.

Take heart, parents; we found this to be a healthy combination of DQ Factor traits in completely normal (relative term), well-balanced children.

6 to 8 (a) answers with approximately 12 or fewer (b) answers

Lower end of the assertive and manipulative end of the Monkey DQ scale. The high (b) range score indicates your child is more of a feel-sorry-for-me type and gets your attention (and therefore, validation of being loved and important) by making you feel guilty.

Any other combination with fewer than 5 (a) answers and 10 or fewer (b) answers

Definitely not a Monkey! Read up about Monkeys in the event you have a Monkey-in-training, then proceed to the next section of the DQ zoo. You will definitely identify your child's or teen's DQ Factor along the tour.

Note: Regardless of the number of (c) answers, they serve only to rule out this DQ Factor and do not have any special significance on their own.

LIFE WITH BART

At the end of each week, my staff would get together to discuss particularly notable families from the previous week. Early on in this process, one family became the standard-bearer for anyone who ever wondered if they were raising a DQ Factor #2—Monkey. Our study family was technically known as Family #81, but to the staff, they were "the Simpsons," named after the animated TV family.

THE SIMPSONS

PARENTS
Mom: Betsy
Dad: Rudy
CHILDREN
T. J. (10)
Justin (8)
Bartholomew (4)

Back at the clinic, our Saturday morning custom was to get together over coffee and bagels (donuts for me, as old cop habits are hard to break) to recap the prior week's DQ activities. Each intern was required to present one case study in each of the four DQ Factors. On a particularly entertaining Saturday, an intern brought the following DQ Factor #2 story to our attention. The intern proceeded to tell us about Bartholomew (nicknamed Bart) and his attention-seeking, manipulative prowess.

The story started with Bart's mom, Betsy, providing Bart and the other children with some last-minute instructions concerning a little get-together she had been planning for several weeks. Betsy was having several ladies over to the house from her Bible study group. On this particular Saturday afternoon, apparently six or seven women were to come to the Simpson home to socialize, drink tea, and play cards. Here is a portion of the conversation that transpired between Betsy and four-year-old Bart at 11:35 A.M. that day.

"Now sweetie, you know that several of the ladies from my church group are coming to the house this afternoon, right, honey?"

"Yeah," responded Bart. (Note to reader: You'll learn very quickly that Bart is a man of action and not conversation.)

Betsy said, "Can I count on you to be on your best behavior? I want you to be a little gentleman and play quietly while Mommy has her friends over. Can you do that for Mommy?

"Yeah." (Again, riveting dialogue.)

"I got you three videos," Betsy continued. "You can watch them in the den while the grownups are playing cards. Can you do that for me, honey?"

Note how Bart's mom speaks down to him in a manner we came to call infantilizing. This term refers to parents who talk down to their child in a placating or pacifying tone of voice. Whenever you catch yourself using a sing-song tone and cadence, you are unconsciously contributing to your child's immaturity. This is especially true when you follow each sentence with a question such as,

"Can you do that for Mommy?" Think about it. Have you ever heard, "Can you do this for Mommy?" only to hear the child reply, "No, I really am not interested in doing it your way"?

As you can imagine, when faced with the can-you-do-this-for-Mommy question, Bart replied, "Yeah."

Now let's fast-forward to 12:20 P.M. as Betsy's friends began to arrive. Everything seemed to be going smoothly. Bart was apparently watching his videos as his mom entertained her guests.

Around 1:00 P.M., Bart entered the living room and stood around the table where the ladies were busily chatting and playing cards. "Mom," he said. (No answer for ten seconds, as you can imagine Bart standing behind his mother's chair, engrossed with her dialogue.)

"Mom." (Again no answer for approximately ten seconds.)

Finally, in a more emphatic and whiny tone that miraculously transforms one-syllable words into multisyllable words, Bart wailed, "MOOMMMM!"

"What is it, sweetie? I told you Mommy was busy and to watch your videos."

"But I don't want to watch videos. I want to watch you play cards."

"I'm sorry, honey," Betsy said. "We talked about this, and you agreed that you were going to be a big boy and watch your videos while Mommy and her friends played cards. Why don't you get yourself a graham cracker and juice and take them back and watch your videos."

Apparently noticing for the first time that Bart was wearing his swimming trunks, floaties, and holding a book on snorkeling, she quizzed, "What are you wearing?"

"I want you to read me a book," Bart said.

"Now you know that I can't read you a book right now, dear. Mommy has her friends over. I know, we'll read a book later this afternoon."

"NO, I WANT TO READ A BOOK NOW!" and with that, Bart proceeded to climb onto his mom's lap.

Clearly getting frustrated, but not wanting to appear out of control in front of her friends, Bart's mom replied in a very controlled tone, "Mommy cannot read you a story right now. Mommy will read you a story later, though. Right now I want you to go to your room and watch your videos."

Our imaginations began to work overtime as we envisioned what was happening next. Starting low and softly as if working up a head of steam, Bart sternly demanded, "No, Mommy. READ ME A STORY NOW!"

Wondering how long it would take for Bart's mom to get firm and insert a boundary, we soon received the answer. "I'll tell you what, sweetie. Why don't you go back to your videos, and if you are a good little man, Mommy will take you out for an ice cream later. Can you do that for Mommy?"

"Yeah."

Betsy excused herself from her group and walked Bart back to the den. While out of the room, we overheard a few of the women commenting on how poorly behaved Bart was. The word *brat* was mentioned, and one woman commented on how she never tolerated such misbehavior with her kids.

After approximately two minutes, Betsy returned to the game stating, "You know, he's just had his little heart set on reading that new book. He just loves to read, and I think it is wonderful that a little guy his age is so interested in books."

Betsy's attempt to brag about Bart after he had thrown a tantrum fell on deaf ears around the table.

Next, according to the transcripts, about eight minutes passed, at which time Bart reentered the living room, apparently naked except for his floaties, and stood behind his mother's chair holding his book.

An unidentified voice said, "Betsy, I think Bart wants you."

"Young man, what is wrong with you?" Betsy exclaimed. "You march yourself right back into your room and do not come out until I tell you to. Now go!"

"But Mommy. You said you would read me my story."

Betsy took Bart back to his room while the dialogue at the table centered around hushed comments about how overly permissive Betsy was and how she had lost control of the little Simpson.

The comment that made us laugh the most came in the form of an elderly voice that was overheard to say, "When I was raising my sons, if one of them had stripped down and paraded around while I was entertaining, I'd have given him a look that would have levitated his little bare behind right back into his room, where I would have introduced it to a wooden spoon. Parents today act as though they are afraid to set down the law."

The woman's comment was endorsed with various affirming comments. Another, less elderly voice commented, "Apparently, Mommy doesn't believe in spanking, and you can see what that gets you."

SUMMARY

Bart and Betsy's interchange provided a classic example of how two personalities mesh to demonstrate a specific DQ Factor in Bart's actions. Bart's first level of acting-out ("Read me a story") stemmed from his desire for attention. In a way, Betsy had unintentionally set him up to act the way he did, as it is unreasonable to believe that a four-year-old would sit quietly and watch videos for three hours.

On top of the setup for failure was the fact that Bart had been conditioned to keep pressing his mom for attention. The history of interaction between the two provided evidence that, whenever he felt he wasn't getting the attention he wanted, Bart would command it by acting out. Even though he received negative attention—a stern warning or led by the hand to his room—attention was still attention. Keep in mind a general observation concerning DQ Factor #2—Monkeys: They typically do not feel good, important, significant, or even particularly loved, unless they are constantly the center of attention. The challenge intensifies when you realize that they are bottomless pits in their need for attention.

Bart, like most of his DQ Monkey colleagues, fits the "cup of water" analogy. Monkeys, by nature, crave attention and will do everything in their power to command it from you. Each time Bart came into the living room, he did so to command attention from his mom, and to some extent he succeeded. Because she was not in a position to give him as much attention as he needed, he found himself back in his room with an empty cup and thirsty for more attention. Each journey back to the group of women provided just enough attention in his cup to last him a short time.

If you could have tuned into Bart's secret thoughts while he impatiently watched videos, you would have recognized some jealousy over the attention his mother was giving to her guests. You would have heard inner thoughts such as: *My mom should be spending time with me.* Or, *I'm not as important to my mom as her group of friends.* Or finally, *I wonder if my mom still loves me?*

With those questions, concerns, and insecurities swirling around his mind, Bart did exactly what many (if not most) children do. They give in to their anxieties and take action to command attention, thereby temporarily assuaging their anxiety. In Bart's case, he knew that stripping down to his birthday suit would provide a more long-lasting attention (and therefore significance) than doing something as common and pedestrian as walking around with a book and floaties.

Attention-seeking behavior annoys parents. When the child is reprimanded, he will usually stop immediately because the attention Band-Aid has been applied. The problem is that the medication in the Band-Aid wears off quickly and the child will frequently begin again later in the same or similar manner. You may recall the earlier example of the daughter who couldn't seem to keep her little Monkey hands (and feet) off the miniblinds. When asked to keep her hands off the blinds, Rachel, desiring attention, may wait a few minutes, then simply resume playing with the blinds with her feet. Inside, she knows she is playing with fire because she has already been scolded for this. But the rationale that she is not using her hands, coupled with her need for attention, easily provides enough motive to risk discipline.

For zookeepers in charge of Monkeys, there are fortunately several effective methods of correcting these behaviors. We will venture deep into these solutions in a moment.

ARE YOU LIVING WITH A MONKEY?

Now it is time to see if you are living with a Monkey. The essential questions below were extracted from the complete DQ Factor battery of tests. Over a period of time, we found that these questions were more than sufficient to fully flush out a child's DQ Factor.

As you did with the previous test, try your best to separate yourself from any emotional investment in the answers or outcome. You can best do this by imagining you are an outsider—but one who knows your child inside and out—and you have been asked to evaluate him or her.

Read the following questions carefully. Each has been designed to correspond to any age child or teenager. Answer the questions below by circling

(a) if you *strongly agree* with the statement,

(b) if you *somewhat agree* with the statement, or

(c) if you *do not agree* with the statement.

DQ FACTOR #2—MONKEY TEST

1. S/he seems to get her/his way far more often than the other children.
   Circle one: (a)   (b)   (c)

2. S/he is quite adept at manipulating you into forgetting what you said about something.
   Circle one: (a)   (b)   (c)

3. When I tell him/her to do his/her chores, it isn't unusual for him/her to start and then get distracted within a few minutes.
   Circle one: (a)   (b)   (c)

4. When it comes to spanking or other discipline, s/he is quite good at talking me out of it.
   Circle one: (a)   (b)   (c)

5. Sometimes I feel like s/he is just a bottomless pit in terms of needing and demanding my attention.
   Circle one: (a)   (b)   (c)

6. I'll ask her/him to bring home school or homework in the morning, just knowing there will be some excuse in the afternoon as to why s/he doesn't have it.
   Circle one: (a)   (b)   (c)

7. S/he is quite skilled at getting me to change my mind.
   Circle one: (a)   (b)   (c)

8. S/he is a great talker and can get you to remove punishment with relative ease.
   Circle one: (a)   (b)   (c)

9. My child is quite social in school and has many friends.
   Circle one: (a)   (b)   (c)

10. My child gets into trouble for talking and goofing around in school.
    Circle one: (a)   (b)   (c)

11. I couldn't imagine my child growing up and working as an accountant or a librarian.
    Circle one: (a)   (b)   (c)

12. My child would choose a group activity over a quiet or solitary activity any time.
    Circle one: (a)   (b)   (c)

13. My child enjoys going places where there is a lot of action, such as arcades or sporting events.
    Circle one: (a)   (b)   (c)

14. My child is more of an optimist than a pessimist.
    Circle one: (a)   (b)   (c)

15. My child could be described more as full of energy than lethargic.
    Circle one: (a)   (b)   (c)

16. If my child were in a school play, s/he would more likely want to have one of the leading roles than one of the supporting roles.
    Circle one: (a)   (b)   (c)

17. My child makes new friends fairly quickly.
    Circle one: (a)   (b)   (c)

18. It isn't unusual for my child to feign sickness to get out of something s/he doesn't want to do, like going to school.
    Circle one: (a)   (b)   (c)

19. I would say my child is more impulsive than calculating.
    Circle one: (a)   (b)   (c)

20. My child is a "drama queen/king," meaning that everything seems to get magnified when it happens to him/her.
    Circle one: (a) (b) (c)

21. Even if s/he did it, my child always seems to have an excuse ready.
    Circle one: (a) (b) (c)

22. My child adapts quickly to new friends and new settings.
    Circle one: (a) (b) (c)

23. My child is more quick and witty than thoughtful and deliberate.
    Circle one: (a) (b) (c)

24. My child may appear insensitive to others, but I know s/he is very sensitive of his/her own feelings and those of others.
    Circle one: (a) (b) (c)

25. It is common for my child to interrupt me in the middle of something I am saying.
    Circle one: (a) (b) (c)

26. My child frequently enters the room talking before checking to see if someone else is talking.
    Circle one: (a) (b) (c)

27. My child is more active than most of his peers.
    Circle one: (a) (b) (c)

28. If s/he paid better attention in class, s/he would do a lot better in school.
    Circle one: (a) (b) (c)

29. My child would prefer playing a video game to reading a book.
    Circle one: (a) (b) (c)

30. Even if s/he stubs her/his toe, s/he works it for all the sympathy s/he can get.
    Circle one: (a)   (b)   (c)

31. I'd say my child is more confident than most other kids his/her age.
    Circle one: (a)   (b)   (c)

32. Putting this child to bed can be a major challenge.
    Circle one: (a)   (b)   (c)

33. S/he learned to walk at a younger age than most.
    Circle one: (a)   (b)   (c)

34. S/he learned to talk at a younger age than most.
    Circle one: (a)   (b)   (c)

35. S/he was more difficult to potty train than my other kids, or more difficult than most kids I've heard about.
    Circle one: (a)   (b)   (c)

36. S/he has a great sense of humor and can make most people laugh.
    Circle one: (a)   (b)   (c)

37. It isn't unusual for him/her to push the limits to the point where I feel like I'm going to explode.
    Circle one: (a)   (b)   (c)

38. Sometimes I wonder if s/he is just sort of daring me to punish her/him.
    Circle one: (a)   (b)   (c)

39. When I catch her/him doing something wrong, I can expect to hear multiple excuses about why it wasn't her/his fault.
    Circle one: (a)   (b)   (c)

40. Sometimes not an hour will pass when I'll find her/him doing the exact same thing I scolded her/him about.
    Circle one: (a)   (b)   (c)

41. S/he plays one parent against the other often.
    Circle one: (a)   (b)   (c)

42. S/he has either myself or my spouse wrapped around his/her little finger.
    Circle one: (a)   (b)   (c)

43. I'll catch her/him asking my spouse if s/he can do something I said no about.
    Circle one: (a)   (b)   (c)

44. I honestly believe this child will just keep it up until s/he gets her/his way.
    Circle one: (a)   (b)   (c)

45. Even though I know it sounds ridiculous, I sometimes believe this child's life mission is to get under my skin and drive me crazy.
    Circle one: (a)   (b)   (c)

46. When I finally have had enough and get angry, s/he acts like nothing has happened.
    Circle one: (a)   (b)   (c)

47. At times I get so frustrated with this child that I can't even remember what it was that made me angry in the first place.
    Circle one: (a)   (b)   (c)

48. When I try to explain to others what it is that frustrates me so much about my child, I find that they just don't seem to understand.
    Circle one: (a)   (b)   (c)

49. When I tell him/her to stop doing something, he/she will figure out a way to get around my boundary and continue.
    Circle one: (a)   (b)   (c)

50. It isn't unusual for me to have to repeat instructions several times before s/he finally does what I tell her/him.
    Circle one: (a)   (b)   (c)

51. If I catch him/her doing something that I know s/he knows is wrong, I can expect a string of excuses.
Circle one: (a)   (b)   (c)

52. If I try to walk away when I'm angry, s/he will likely follow me.
Circle one: (a)   (b)   (c)

SCORING YOUR DQ FACTOR #2—MONKEY TEST

Add up the number of (a) answers and put the number here: _____

Add up the number of (b) answers and put the number here: _____

Add up the number of (c) answers and put the number here: _____

INTERPRETING YOUR CHILD'S/TEENAGER'S DQ #2 TEST

Total number of questions   52

42 or more (a) answers with approximately 10 (b) answers

As a precursor, it is important to keep these scores in perspective. If your child or teenager scored high in this DQ Factor, be careful not to leap to conclusions. High scores do not translate into emotional or psychological problems, nor are they an indicator of intelligence. They are merely a correlation of the type of discipline your child will respond to best.

Very high on the manipulative DQ scale for a Monkey. Whenever a score of 40+ shows up on this test, you are often dealing with a child who has experienced losses. Whether it is through divorce, death, or multiple relocations in residence, these children often have a sense of insecurity that drives their need to challenge you for attention. It is this same insecurity, however, that keeps them from being as aggressive as their DQ Bear counterparts.

By intelligence measurement standards, children and teenagers in this group tested high. The real surprise was that they tested off-the-chart high in an area called *intrapersonal intelligence*. A high score in this category indicates a superior sense of what they are feeling inside. Children who score high in this area are often very sensitive and sometimes moody. On the other hand, they also tend to be very caring and loving souls.

29 to 41 (a) answers with approximately 20 (b) answers

Moderately high Monkey DQ Factor. This child is definitely out to get your attention, like the child who scores 42 and above. The main difference is that this child has likely not experienced the degree of loss and therefore is not as needy and blatantly manipulative as the other.

The 29 to 41 range in this DQ Factor featured kids who scored in the upper third of IQ testing we conducted.

19 to 28 (a) answers with approximately 10 (b) answers

Moderate DQ Factor for the average Monkey. This DQ Factor, in this range, tends to be somewhat more manipulative and indirect in the way he communicates. Oddly enough, children and teenagers in this particular range tended to lie more frequently than any other Monkey DQ level. In fact, this subset of DQ Factor #2 featured the highest level of lying among all DQ Factor types. Stranger still, the lies told by this particular group were found to be of a silly, meaningless variety that would cause us to shake our heads and try to determine why he or she felt the need to lie at all.

Lying is often a conditioned and sometimes near-involuntary result of strong insecurities. Whenever kids scored in this particular range, we looked specifically for strong, controlling parents who tended to be more my-way-

or-the-highway types, or kids who were very insecure for any number of other reasons.

---

12 to 18 (a) answers with approximately 8 to 10 (b) answers

Low to moderate range. These kids were found to be less insecure than the kids who scored in the range above, and they did not struggle to tell the truth nearly as much.

Overall, we determined children and teenagers with a total in this range to be (gulp) normal—whatever that means—in security/insecurity issues and levels of independence and neediness. They had good relationships and got along well with almost everyone.

---

11 or fewer (a) answers with 8 or fewer (b) answers

Definitely not a Monkey. If you already ruled out DQ Factor #1—Bears as well, then you are likely going to find your child in one (or both) of the next DQ Factors.

Note: Regardless of the number of (c) answers, they serve only to rule out this DQ Factor and do not have any special significance on their own.

THE DQ RX FOR MONKEYS

As previously stated, there is a lengthy continuum of disciplinary techniques available to parents when their child has broken a rule or stepped over a boundary. One of the primary objectives of the study was to focus on and identify both the ineffective and effective disciplinary techniques used with specific DQ Factors. My team and I found it remarkable that the majority of parents repeatedly utilized nearly identical methods of discipline—even when that discipline proved to be ineffective.

The list below comprises the disciplinary methods most frequently used by parents of Monkeys. The list is separated by type of discipline and effectiveness. In this situation, effectiveness refers to both an objective and subjective percentage we assigned to each discipline form as we witnessed its implementation and overall success rate in creating behavioral changes among DQ Factor #2—Monkeys.

Type of Discipline with DQ Factor #2—Monkeys	Effectiveness
AGGRESSIVE SPANKING	21 PERCENT

This term refers to any spanking technique that ranged from taking the child's pants down, to spanking him with an open palm, to utilizing a spanking instrument such as a wooden spoon, wooden hanger, paddle, etc.

Note: There were no abuse issues throughout the study. Societal standards still view spanking with objects that do not leave permanent marks to be acceptable. For the record, I am not opposed to spanking, but I am opposed to using any instrument (spoons, hangers, belts, etc.) to spank children. Utilizing these items can clearly inflict excessive and unintentional injury.

SIMPLE SWATTING	36 PERCENT

This term refers to a spanking technique that would be called a simple swat (or series of swats) to the child's buttocks, delivered by the hand to the outside of the pants and/or underwear.

IGNORING   78 PERCENT

Ignoring is the premeditated practice of
not letting your child's attention-seeking
misbehaviors get to you. For instance,
when your child acts out in a clear effort
to get your attention, the rule of ignoring
simply states to continue doing what you
are doing. Don't let your child see that
he has gotten to you or he will continue
to pull the strings and you will continue
to do your little puppet dance.

Ignoring also requires you to be in control
of your nonverbal signals (facial expressions,
sighs, groans, etc.). I liken this approach to
being confronted by a strange dog (no
offense intended with the analogy) who
snarls at you. If you show signs of fear or
you run, you are meat. Likewise, sending
your DQ Factor Monkey verbal and
nonverbal signals that he is getting to you
during the ignoring process will immediately
nullify its desired effects.

VERBAL REPRIMANDS   29 PERCENT

This form of discipline did not work
effectively with Monkeys for a number
of reasons. Primarily though, it was
because the verbal reprimand
accomplished their objective of getting
attention. On top of that, the reprimand
(put-down) triggered more insecurities,
which caused this DQ actor to act out
even more to garner attention.

TIME-OUTS   83 PERCENT

Monkey DQ Factor types are highly
social creatures. Therefore, removing a

Monkey from outside stimuli through time-outs in his room proved highly effective. The reason it works so well is that he is seeking attention through misbehavior. When his attention-seeking actions result in isolation (the opposite of attention), he is forced to deal with his needs in more appropriate ways.

RESTRICTIONS

58 PERCENT

Restrictions in this decade seem to be the grown-up big brother of time-outs. Whereas a time-out was generally limited to less than a half-hour in the child's room, we found that restrictions averaged 24 hours. We also found that restrictions commonly started out as longer terms (48 to 72 hours in the room, not going out, in bed by 8:00 P.M., etc.), but were commuted (reduced) as the talented Monkey pleaded his case before the judge.

Parents (especially parents of this DQ Factor) who set longer restriction periods of three to five days of loss of privileges—and then followed through—were much more apt to gain compliance later.

We noted that Monkeys detested, but later became much more compliant with, parental rules when they experienced restrictions of two to four hours of time-out confinement to their rooms. That translated into coming out for meals, homework, or after-school sporting activities and the like. Afterward, however, they were back in their rooms until their time was up.

Parents who restricted their kids to their rooms for periods of three to seven days experienced more acting-out behaviors both during and after the punishment. The rationale behind this seemed to be that the alienation (separation) from the family created too many insecurities, which then caused the child to act out to garner more attention.

TAKING AWAY PRIVILEGES

68 PERCENT

Taking away privileges such as TV, stereo, or bike proved to be an effective tool for parents of Monkeys. Because this DQ Factor relies so heavily on outside stimuli to stay busy, removing important things following a behavior problem served as a reminder for future violations.

The second reason that taking away privileges was as effective as it was stemmed from its connection to natural consequences. For example, if your two children were fighting over who gets control over the TV remote (clearly, two boys), then calmly unplugging the TV would serve as both a removal of a privilege as well as a natural consequence. Keep in mind that the key is to do all of this in a calm, matter-of-fact manner.

BELITTLING

NO REGISTERED EFFECTIVENESS

Completely ineffective! If you set out to destroy your child's emotional security and sense of well-being (especially among DQ Factor Monkeys), belittling would definitely be your first choice.

Perhaps only second to intimidating techniques, this form of discipline is destined to lead to increased immediate conduct problems, as well as more serious future conflicts.

THREATS   19 PERCENT

Making a threat is something parents do when they know they are weak when it comes to consequences. We discovered that parents of DQ Factor Monkeys often found themselves feeling trapped and at their wit's end. These feelings caused them to resort to making threats in an attempt to get their kids to comply and behave.

We found another common thread running through these parents as well. They tended to make threats and then neglect to enforce the consequences. This scenario caused the children to disregard not only future threats, but legitimate requests. Keep in mind that a boundary is only a request if it does not have a communicated, understood, and fully anticipated potential for consequences.

NATURAL CONSEQUENCES   76 PERCENT

Natural consequences likely produce such positive results because they are based on how God and the universe function. The Bible is very clear in presenting God's laws of consequences. He states the rules upfront (in black and white) that we are free to choose any course we desire, but there are natural consequences (both positive and negative)

to our choices. The sooner we can transform
our children's choice-processing skills to the
point where they weigh consequences,
the better. Please refer to the Rx #1 below
to discover more about the power of implementing natural consequences.

THE DQ RX

In addition to the insights gained by examining the aforementioned typical
types of discipline used in conjunction with DQ Factor Monkeys, our research
also produced some other effective boundary and discipline techniques. We
found the following Rx actions and ideas to be powerful in neutralizing those
pesky little misbehaving characteristics of Monkeys.

Rx #1
NATURAL CONSEQUENCES

With natural consequences, the child experiences the inevitable results of his own
actions. For example, if the child continues to play with his toys even though
you have called him to come to dinner several times, the natural consequence
is that his dinner will get cold. Natural consequences are best understood as
the consequence of the child's action *without* parental intervention. You would
be shocked how often we parents intervene to prevent our kids from having to
endure the consequences of their actions.

The parents of an eight-year-old came to me in search of solutions for
helping their daughter to get dressed and ready for school on time. She routinely
sat around in her pajamas either watching TV, reading a story, eating cereal, or
playing with her dolls. The parents had tried everything from taking away privileges
to bribes to restrictions. Nothing seemed to motivate her to get dressed and
ready for school on time.

By coaching the parents through the natural consequence (NC) theory, I led them to the conclusion that, in this case, their daughter's NC would be to go to school in her pajamas. As is often the case, both parents stated that they had warned their daughter that they would do exactly that several times before. Obviously, all they had accomplished through idle threats was to communicate to her that they were not serious about her stopping the misbehavior. Rule number one of all DQ Factor discipline techniques is: Follow through on stated consequences or they mean nothing.

I instructed them to write down on a piece of paper (in eight-year-old terms) that they were not going to permit her to stall around before school any longer. I also told them to put the note on her pillow and put a Hershey's chocolate kiss on top of the note. The reason for this tactic is that seeing it in writing produces a message with greater impact than trying to get a child to listen to one more scolding. The note communicated a clear-cut boundary. Since it was in writing, it was for real—like a contract. The chocolate sent the message that they loved her and didn't want the message to be misconstrued as anything but a loving boundary.

The note read:

Dear Shannon:

We want to help motivate you to get ready to go to school on time each morning.
We want you to understand that, starting tomorrow morning, if you are not dressed and
ready to leave the house by 8:10 A.M., we will take you to school in whatever you are wearing.
We love you and know you can get ready on time if you choose to.
Mom and Dad

The following morning, Shannon was still in her pajamas at 8:10 A.M. Her mother calmly took her by the hand and led her to the car and drove her to school. Shannon cried all the way to school and stopped only when her mother produced her school clothes in a bag. She calmly instructed Shannon that she would allow her to change in the car *this time*, but hereafter, she would not bring a change of clothes with her and she would insist that Shannon go to her classroom in her pajamas.

In case you are wondering, Shannon was up, dressed, and ready to leave the house by 7:50 A.M. every day the next week, and the last time I spoke with the parents (some six months later), Shannon was still quite punctual.

As far as those of you who may be thinking that this technique could have scarred her little psyche for life, I respectfully and clinically reply, "Give me a break." Letting your child experience the natural consequences of his or her misbehavior is one of the most effective discipline tools you have in your toolbox.

As a word of caution, NCs are not available in every misbehaving circumstance. If your child particularly enjoys licking wall sockets (please tell me this is not your teenager), an incorrect natural consequence would be to pull up a chair, grab some popcorn, and watch his or her hair become naturally curly. You cannot resort to NCs when the outcome could be dangerous. In these instances, you need to move to a *logical consequence*.

Rx #2
LOGICAL CONSEQUENCES

Logical consequences are the disciplinary techniques you employ when the natural consequences could lead to danger. For instance, if your child rides his tricycle in the street after you have warned him, then you simply follow the path to the logical consequence of taking his tricycle away for the day.

Rx #3

Disregarding

Disregarding is a powerful psychological tool that most parents don't even know about. It also happens to be perhaps the best technique to use with Monkeys.

The theory behind disregarding is that if a behavior is not reinforced (at least occasionally), it will decrease and then die under its own weight. Keep in mind that even negative reinforcement (criticism, yelling, punishment) is reinforcement.

The trick to disregarding is that you must practice it each time the behavior occurs if you want it to go away. Let me give you an example among older kids, teenagers, and adults. Let's say there is a temperamental vending machine at your office. At least half of the time after you've inserted your dollar bill (for a fifty-cent candy bar) into the machine, it does nothing. No movement, no candy bar. You push the change return button a few times with nothing to show for it. Resorting to violence, you kick the bottom of the machine, push the change button two hundred more times, push your selection a couple more times, but again, nothing.

When the machine refuses to give the merchandise or return your money, you will eventually give up. However, if after your abusive tirade against the machine, it had coughed up either your money or your candy bar, you could bet your life that you would kick and poke that machine every time you had a problem with it—maybe even for fun on Fridays. Why? Because you would have assumed that your candy-dislodging actions had worked.

Now apply this with a three-year-old. Let's say he has picked up a nasty little disturbing addition to his four-letter vocabulary (not from you, of course). Needless to say, you would prefer his new word not be broadcast each time you have company, let alone to his Sunday school teacher. You could swat his hand each time he says it or try some other form of discipline, but at some point he is going to figure out this is a way to get you to pay attention to him. You might consider this approach instead.

Step 1

Before he says it again, remind him that you do not like that word, it isn't something that nice boys say, and you do not want him to use that word again. Ask him if he understands and will do his best to comply.

Step 2

When you hear the word again (and you will hear it again), you must calmly reinforce that you had hoped you would not hear that word ever coming from him again. Let him know that you will not talk to him when he is using words like that.

Step 3

When you hear the word again (yes, your Monkey will test you again), you must *disregard* it. Do not get mad, don't punish him, don't shriek and run from the room; just ignore it and go about your business. Don't even make eye contact. If he asks you if you heard what he said, calmly reply that you did and that you told him you would not talk to him when he is using such words.

Monkey DQ Factor types will nearly always attempt to get the desired response from you by increasing the intensity of their actions. If the child whines, he may whine more loudly or persistently than before, hoping to get the predicted response. If you can remain unresponsive, the inappropriate behavior will eventually die out.

Rx#4

SUBSTITUTION

Among younger DQ Factor Monkeys, we found that a technique called *substitution* was often effective—especially among parents who had difficulty disregarding whining or crying behavior. This involves distracting your child's attention away from the problematic behavior by substituting a similar, more appropriate behavior for the one that is inappropriate.

For instance, your four-year-old insists on reaching up to the top of the stove. You've tried swatting his hand, and that just made a game out of it. Obviously you aren't going to let him experience the natural consequences, and other techniques just don't seem to get the job done. Substitution means you evaluate why he is so attracted to the top of the stove. It is likely that this is where your attention is directed, and he wants your attention. It could also be that there are interesting bright pans up there and they look like fun.

So you should take a couple of pans from the cupboard and place them on the floor away from the stove. Next, take a wooden spoon (not the same one you use for spankings, please) and make-believe you are cooking. Don't even invite him over to help. Just make it look like it is *very* fun, and he will come over and want to play too. Hand him the spoon and then compliment him on the wonderful job he is doing in preparing the imaginary dinner. Now you can return to your cooking. If he comes back to the stove, tell him that you cannot cook with him there, but redirect him to his pots and pans on the floor.

Oh, and just in case you were confused about the wooden spoon comment above, I do not recommend using any objects to spank children. If you do spank, an open palm to the bottom has been the attention-grabber of choice for centuries.

Rx #5

Catching 'Em in the Act!

It has been said that for every negative comment or reprimand you toss your child's way, you should say seven positive things to counteract it. I'm not sure about the math, but it seems some of us would be up all night trying to come up with positive statement number 735. Eventually we'd be down to things like, "You don't seem to sweat much for a six-year-old."

On a more serious note, it is highly beneficial for all DQ Factors—but especially for Monkeys—that their parents provide frequent compliments. I call it *catching them in the act of doing something right!* You'd be surprised how often you can do just that. The more frequently you can compliment your child for behaving well in a situation where he normally misbehaves, the more likely he will be to repeat the right behavior.

Rx #6

Putting Your Monkey to Work (The Deck of Chores)

You may recall our discussion of The Deck of Chores and how effective it was with Bear DQ Factors. It was equally worthy with Monkeys.

This is the clever idea that employs between ten and fifty blank four-by-six cards. On each card write a different chore on one side and the card number on the reverse. Make sure you write age-appropriate chores for your child so you do not have your five-year-old up on the roof with your pneumatic hammer, replacing the shingles.

When your child misbehaves and it is time to decide on his discipline, we found that a visit to The Deck of Chores was both entertaining and effective, but it did something for each DQ Factor that we had not anticipated. Because the child was the one to select a discipline chore from the deck, he could not really blame the parent for making him do something he hated to do. Remember, Monkeys are champion blamers. If he chooses it, he's stuck with his decision.

Rx #7
REFLECTIVE LISTENING

Having a win-at-all-costs mentality to confronting discipline will blow up in your face with most people, but especially among Monkeys. Winning is too often the goal of both parent and Monkey throughout the discipline process, and it nearly always leads to more problems. Each one has a point to make and wants the other to acknowledge it.

The fine art of reflective listening requires you to listen and reflect back to your child what you hear from him or her. This marvelous technique

    a)   slows the conversation down to a manageable pace,

    b)   requires you to listen, and

    c)   better allows your child to hear what he is saying, as it is coming from someone other than himself.

A reflective listening technique would sound something like this:

"So Matt, if I am hearing you right, you are saying you think it is unfair that I don't let you go shoot paintballs with David and Tim today. And your point is that, even though I think there needs to be parental supervision, you think they are very safe on their own. Is that your basic view?"

As you can see, reflective listening boils down everything to just the issue at hand. It also puts the issue in succinct and focused terms that facilitate a solution rather than allowing it to take on a life of its own into unrelated matters.

A Final View of the Monkey Zoo

I've often thought that a Parents of Monkeys support group would be a huge idea and potential moneymaker. The Prozac concession stand alone would turn millions in profit.

As lovable as they are cute, Monkeys are the most tenacious of the DQ Factors. They will keep after you, wear you down, and grind you to a stump— all the while being truly adorable.

Monkey DQs are really special children. They are fun and exciting, and there is never a dull moment around them. Hopefully the advice and the success quotients attached to disciplinary techniques will help you handle your pet. If not, there is an opening on Saturday mornings at the Prozac stand.

CHAPTER 8

DQ FACTOR #3—PORCUPINES
(THE REVENGE-SEEKERS IN THE ZOO)

Your tour of the DQ zoo has reached its halfway mark. Just to retrace our steps, we visited the Bear (DQ Factor #1) compound and took a close look at how his need to feel important and significant drives him to misbehave and challenge you for control and authority.

Next we cruised through the Monkey (DQ Factor #2) enclosure for a close-up view of these cute, strong-willed little critters that get their primary sense of importance and significance by demanding all of your attention. Monkeys really feel the most significant when they have your complete attention, and they will stop at little to get it.

PORCUPINES AND YELLOW CARDS

Let's take a quick break from our tour of the DQ zoo to visit a zoo of a different color—my son's high school. In fact, I actually had somewhat of a DQ epiphany while watching Matthew play on his varsity soccer team and observing how a soccer team mirrors the family system.

For starters a team, like a family, is made up of individuals, each of whom interacts among members of the group while struggling to establish an identity. The soccer team has a coach who, like a parent, is trying to maintain control, gently encourage, and motivate his kids to achieve. The soccer model also has an ultimate authority figure on the field: the referee. The family's ultimate authority figure is usually the father. The difference, however, is that the soccer authority figure wears a strange-looking outfit (bumblebee colors), whereas the home authority figure gets to wear normal clothing. The analogies go on and on, but the last one for us to look at is that soccer has field rules, just like the family has house rules.

To digress momentarily, I found it particularly interesting when watching two of the players on the field going at it. I mean, here you have two zit-producing testosterone factories bumping, kicking, scratching, pulling each other's shorts, and calling each other words that make you wonder if they ever kissed their mommies goodnight with those mouths. They are, in similar ways, searching for significance, attention, and a sense of belonging. Then the greatest thing happens. The referee, in black knee-highs, blows his whistle, and everybody stops and stares at him. He, too, has found his significance. And no offense, but does anybody but me look at soccer refs and think that the only place these guys ever find significance is when they are running up and down the field in their yellow-and-black bumblebee outfits, blowing their whistles at kids? You have to figure that Monday through Friday these same poor guys sit in a three-by-three-foot cubicle taking orders from sixty-three supervisors, including the night janitor. Ah, but on the weekend they are truly significant, and as Shakespeare (might have) said, Significance by any other name would smell as sweet.

Back to the two combatant players who are still shooting each other snotty-faced looks and calling each other "girls" in an adolescent attempt to find significance in the eyes of their peers. And here comes our bumblebee ultimate authority figure, marching—no, make that goosestepping (á la the Third Reich)—

to the middle of the field where our two boys are standing. Almost magically the two combatants assume angelic, Mother Teresa-like poses as if to say, "Why, whatever do you mean, sir?"

And the comparison to the family doesn't end there. The referee opens his shirt pocket and produces a magical card—a magical yellow card, which I suppose is the only and best color for magical cards. Then he holds this card up like it just came out of the ark of the covenant and shows it to the two boys and then to the coaches and parents. Amazing. The two boys just turn and walk directly to their sidelines without saying a word. It's as if the magic card renders teenage boys in shinguards mute before sending them to their rooms—or sidelines.

Later I had to ask what was written on the magical yellow card that produces so much fear and trembling in the hearts of teenage boys. I mean, what would cause them to fall instantly silent and passively go to their places? Whatever it had on it, I had to know. Every parent, teacher, cop, and social worker had to have one of these magic yellow cards in his or her shirt pocket. I imagined it contained some mystical or biblical caution. Perhaps an incantation, or better still, a picture of a teenager being drawn and quartered on a medieval rack. To my shock, I learned that the yellow card was just that—a plain yellow card. Not even a bloodstain to serve as a warning of what happened to the last soccer player who didn't bow and then leave the field quietly and quickly.

And then the epiphany struck! Since the card held no magic value, that meant that the power came from the *holder* of the yellow card—the bumblebee ultimate authority figure on the field. And the authority came in the way of a promise that if the two players didn't walk directly and quietly to their respective sidelines, then there was an even more powerful card in his pocket—THE RED CARD! Therefore, the fabled and magical yellow card was the warning that better produce the desired result, or the dreaded RED CARD would be paying a visit.

FORWARDS, FULLBACKS, AND DQ FACTORS

Okay, let's take the soccer analogy one more step. While watching my son's soccer game, I was struck by how easy it is to spot the various DQ Factor types by the way they play the game. Because I don't know the boys or their off-field personalities, I began to form DQ conclusions about what they were like based on their on-field personas. The players whom I identified as DQ Factor #1—Bears were the quickest to get yellow cards. They bristled at the challenges of other players, and even the referees. Some Bears even challenged their coaches when they felt they were being challenged back. Their drive to feel and be seen as *significant* caused them to display an aggressive style of play.

DQ Factor #2—Monkeys were all over the field. They were the tenacious, animated hustlers who seemed to be the center of (you guessed it) *attention*. They were vocal and sometimes found themselves being drawn out of position because of their desire to be around the ball. Again, the ball was the center of attention, so these players wanted to be near it all the time.

DQ Factor #3—Porcupines should avoid headers at all costs. (For those of you who don't know soccer, that is a joke about how their quills would pop the ball.) Porcupines were more difficult to spot. They seemed to be away from the action more often than not, and if this DQ Factor got a yellow card, you can bet it was a revenge move. For example, I was watching one particular player on my son's team. He is a very nice Christian boy who comes across as mild-tempered and respectful. He was guarding a very aggressive, DQ Bear-type player on the opposing team. On one particular play, the opposing player did a move called a slide tackle and took our player down. It was not a clean play, but the referee did not call a penalty. Our player did not say a word, but I made a point to watch him for the next ten minutes even though the ball may have been at the other end of the field. Sure enough, a good eight minutes later, he elbowed the player who had tackled him. When the other team's player retaliated, our Porcupine smartly walked away. Seeing this, the referee called a penalty against the other team. Porcupine DQ Factors *never forget*. When you make them look bad, hurt them, or do something to reduce their sense of significance, sooner or later they will pay you back.

Even though we haven't covered DQ Factor #4—Lambs to any extent, I will tell you that you don't tend to see this Factor on the soccer field at the upper levels of competition. You will see all sorts of Lambs on youth soccer fields, but they tend to self-eliminate as they get older. This is because Lambs tend to be *defeatists*. They are not competitive DQ types, and they don't see themselves as capable. They tend to avoid direct comparisons to others because it serves to erode their sense of self-importance. Lambs are the kids you have to force to play just so they will get some exercise and socialization through team athletics.

A Concluding Thought

I think I have taken this analogy about as far as I can. DQ Factor #3—Porcupines, like soccer players on the field, are searching for self-importance, significance, and self-worth. They will sometimes say and do angry, hurtful things like swearing, demeaning, and hurting your feelings in a miscalculated attempt to elevate their self-image.

I can illustrate it best by a comment I made to my father when I was a fourteen-year-old DQ Factor #3 working as a box boy (I think the socially acceptable term these days is clerk's helper) at a local supermarket. Because I was too young to drive, my mom would drive me to work after school and my dad would pick me up at 10:30 P.M. I must have had a horrible day because when my dad picked me up, I was not in a good mood. My dad, a successful executive with Kellogg Company, tended to be somewhat of a perfectionistic nagger who, although he always wanted the best for me, pushed me a bit too hard at times. As I recall the incident, he said something about my needing to go to college so I could do more than just work in a grocery store. In a typical Porcupine DQ manner, I snapped back, "Do you mean so I don't end up selling cereal my whole life like you?"

He didn't say a word. He just drove me home in silence, which was the worst possible punishment I could have received. Even thirty years later, I still feel pangs of guilt about saying such a mean thing to my dad, even though I apologized several times later. This was a typically hurtful comment made by an inwardly angry Porcupine. When a Porcupine feels criticized, put down, or minimized, he will *always* pay you back. His delicate balance of self-worth cannot tolerate a direct hit, and the only way for him to recoup a sense of importance is to elevate himself by pulling you down. Again, words are the weapon of choice, although Porcupines tend to be fighters too.

Oh, and in case you were wondering why we started calling DQ Factor #3 *Porcupines*, it is because of the number of relatable comparisons between the animal and the DQ Factor.

Both Porcupines (animals and DQ Factor #3) are very complex and defensive-minded creatures. As a DQ Factor, Porcupines aren't as aggressive as Bears— they aren't out challenging you for control as a way to feel significant. Likewise, Porcupines differ from Monkeys in that they are not commanding or demanding your constant attention in order to feel significant. When they are not on a revenge mission to pay you back for something you did, the children and teenagers who score high in this DQ Factor are usually more on the subdued, quiet, private, sensitive, intelligent, and introspective personality side.

The porcupine's quills provide a wonderful literal and figurative connection to our DQ Factor as well. On the outside, the porcupine looks menacing. The quills are there as a deterrent, but you can actually pet them—just as long as you pet them in the right direction. If you rile a porcupine up or it senses danger, the porcupine raises its quills in a defensive posture to keep attackers at bay. This goes for both the animal and the DQ Factor.

Like his namesake, the human equivalent DQ Factor also tends to be nonaggressive and defensive-minded. These children and teenagers don't make a habit of provoking battles of words, wits, or strength. However, when then feel they have been criticized, put down, minimized, or are not getting the love they need to be significant, out come the quills—and a double dose of retaliation is headed your way. If hurt and feeling insignificant, rest assured this DQ type will hold a grudge and pursue a course of revenge until he has regained his sense of significance.

So now that we have identified Porcupines as the DQ Factor that is motivated toward revenge when their sense of self-worth and significance is damaged, we can move on to diagnosing whether you have one of these little critters in your home.

Are You Experiencing a Porcupine in Your Zoo?

Below is a primary list of feelings that parents experience most frequently throughout the misbehaving—discipline—resolution process. To remind you how to get started in the diagnosis process, let's go back to the technique called *projected visualization*.

Step 1
Close your eyes and clear your head for one minute by trying not to think about anything. Try just focusing your mind's eye on a blank wall that has been painted light blue.

Step 2

Now think back to the last significant misbehaving episode with your child and relive all the various feelings you felt when you discovered the misbehavior, all the way up to the time you resolved it. Relive just those feelings for one full minute.

Step 3

Now take all of those thoughts and feelings and sum them up in one or two words that best describe your emotions at the time.

Step 4

Now search the list of emotions below to see if any of these emotions match (or come close to) the emotions you last experienced while your child was misbehaving. The highlighted section contains the words most commonly used by parents of Porcupines to describe their disciplinary feelings.

PERC (Parent's Emotional Response Chart)
For use in determining child's DQ Factor

DQ Factor #1 — Bears

Threatened

Challenged

Angry

DQ Factor #2 — Monkeys

Irritated

Annoyed

Controlled

DQ FACTOR #3—PORCUPINES

Hurt

Manipulated

Minimized

DQ FACTOR #4—LAMBS

Inadequate

Pity

Frustrated

If you found any of your answers under DQ Factor #3—Porcupines, then you have your first affirmative indication that your child or teenager may be of this DQ Factor.

Just as you used the earlier test to determine if you are living with a Bear or a Monkey, take a few moments to collect your thoughts and take the DQ Factor #3—Porcupine FED-UP test. As you do so, continue (as you did above) to monitor your feelings in regard to your child's last misbehaving episode. Tune in particularly to how you felt during and after the disciplinary process. By paying attention to your feelings, the FED-UP test should help you in diagnosing your child's specific DQ Factor.

PARENT FEELING EVALUATION FOR DQ FACTOR #3 TEST

Try to just relax as you answer the following questions. It may be easier to do so if you acknowledge that there are no right or wrong answers; there is no judgment or preconceived reflections on you as a parent based on any of the answers. It is designed only to provide you with information.

FED-UP INSTRUCTIONS

There is a particular frame of mind that I routinely ask parents to engage in before they take any test regarding their children or their parenting skills. That mind-set is to try, as best you can, to separate yourself from being defensive of your own parenting skills. None of us, especially me, is a natural parent. I'm certain that if you got my teenagers alone in a room for an hour, they could think of at least one mistake I've made with them this year (humor and not narcissism).

The key to this test is to try to be as objective as you can in your answers. Likewise, don't be concerned with how you perceive the test is going for your child. No one but you and your spouse should ever see the results from this test, so it does no good to try to make it look better. The value of this test is in determining a *true* score and not a *hopeful* one.

Read the following questions carefully. Each has been designed to correspond to both children as well as teenagers. Sometimes it is helpful to answer the questions while imagining that you are actually someone else, but someone who knows every intimate detail about you and your family. Answer the questions by circling

(a) if you *strongly agree* with the statement,

(b) if you *somewhat agree* with the statement, or

(c) if you *do not agree* with the statement.

DQ FACTOR #3—PORCUPINE FED-UP TEST
(FEELINGS EXPERIENCED DURING UNRULY PERIODS)

When my child or teenager misbehaves and I confront the behavior with discipline, I feel the following:

1. I find myself just feeling hurt by things s/he says to me.
   Circle one:　　(a)　　　(b)　　　(c)

2. I can't understand why s/he treats me this way.
   Circle one: (a)   (b)   (c)

---

3. I can't believe this is the way I am repaid after all I have done for him/her.
   Circle one: (a)   (b)   (c)

---

4. Even though I'm the parent, I feel as though I never get the last word.
   Circle one: (a)   (b)   (c)

---

5. Sometimes I get the sense that s/he has little respect for me.
   Circle one: (a)   (b)   (c)

---

6. I feel that s/he says these things to get back at me for something.
   Circle one: (a)   (b)   (c)

---

7. I feel that s/he takes her/his anger out on me because I will take it.
   Circle one: (a)   (b)   (c)

---

8. When I punish my child, s/he acts as though it doesn't bother her/him at all.
   Circle one: (a)   (b)   (c)

---

9. Sometimes s/he will do things to get under my skin.
   Circle one: (a)   (b)   (c)

---

10. I sometimes feel that s/he is the least cooperative child I know.
    Circle one: (a)   (b)   (c)

---

11. I feel more angry than hurt when s/he says or does hurtful things to me.
    Circle one: (a)   (b)   (c)

---

12. Even though I know I don't deserve this type of behavior, I somehow come away feeling like it was my fault.
    Circle one: (a)   (b)   (c)

13. I have found myself stunned and almost speechless by something hurtful s/he has said to me.
    Circle one: (a)   (b)   (c)

14. I get confused sometimes and don't know how to respond when s/he misbehaves.
    Circle one: (a)   (b)   (c)

15. I wish I had some magic pill that would make my child easier to manage.
    Circle one: (a)   (b)   (c)

16. I have a tough time keeping a positive perspective when it comes to my child's misbehaving ways.
    Circle one: (a)   (b)   (c)

17. Even though I try not to, I find that I get pulled into exchanging angry words with my child.
    Circle one: (a)   (b)   (c)

18. In a battle of wills, I sometimes feel as though I am going to lose.
    Circle one: (a)   (b)   (c)

19. When my child misbehaves, I get the feeling s/he is doing it to get back at me or someone else.
    Circle one: (a)   (b)   (c)

20. Even though I feel angry when s/he misbehaves, I think I am really more hurt than angry.
    Circle one: (a)   (b)   (c)

21. Sometimes I find myself thinking or saying, "How can you do this to me?"
    Circle one: (a)   (b)   (c)

22. I worry that, away from home, my child doesn't feel like s/he "fits in."
    Circle one: (a)   (b)   (c)

23. I know this sounds strange, but I find myself giving in to something that I don't feel good about, just to avoid having to deal with him/her.
    Circle one: (a)   (b)   (c)

24. I get confused with why s/he is so angry at me when I haven't done anything.
    Circle one: (a)   (b)   (c)

25. Sometimes I just think s/he knows how to go right for the jugular.
    Circle one: (a)   (b)   (c)

26. Just when I think s/he is over it, s/he will say or do something that convinces me that s/he isn't.
    Circle one: (a)   (b)   (c)

27. Sometimes I just feel so minimized.
    Circle one: (a)   (b)   (c)

28. This child/teen can hold on to anger longer than I could imagine.
    Circle one: (a)   (b)   (c)

29. I've had to apologize to others for things my child has said to them.
    Circle one: (a)   (b)   (c)

30. I feel like my child needs some space when s/he is angry.
    Circle one: (a)   (b)   (c)

31. It surprises me when my child will be angry for something that happened hours or even days ago.
    Circle one: (a)   (b)   (c)

32. Sometimes I worry that my child has more of a temper than s/he should have.
    Circle one: (a)   (b)   (c)

33. I feel as though I have a long fuse when it comes to dealing with my child's misbehavior.
Circle one: (a)   (b)   (c)

34. At times, I feel like I am inadequate as a parent.
Circle one: (a)   (b)   (c)

35. I think other parents have an easier time with their child(ren) than I do.
Circle one: (a)   (b)   (c)

36. I sometimes feel like I've been too harsh with him/her, but I didn't know any other way to get him/her to understand my point.
Circle one: (a)   (b)   (c)

37. I've felt the sting of him/her saying some very hurtful things to me.
Circle one: (a)   (b)   (c)

38. I've worried that s/he is a bit cold-hearted.
Circle one: (a)   (b)   (c)

39. On occasion, I feel like s/he is in control and that I have lost control.
Circle one: (a)   (b)   (c)

40. S/he challenges me more than s/he does my spouse.
Circle one: (a)   (b)   (c)

41. I seem to bear the brunt of his/her frustration over situations that I am not even responsible for.
Circle one: (a)   (b)   (c)

42. I worry that s/he obsesses about a person or people who have hurt her/his feelings.
Circle one: (a)   (b)   (c)

SCORING YOUR DQ FACTOR #3—PORCUPINE FED-UP TEST

Add up the number of (a) answers and put the number here: ＿＿＿

Add up the number of (b) answers and put the number here: ＿＿＿

Add up the number of (c) answers and put the number here: ＿＿＿

INTERPRETING YOUR DQ FACTOR #3—PORCUPINE FED-UP TEST

Total number of questions   42

31 or more (a) answers with approximately 10 (b) answers

Wait until the results are in for the expanded Porcupine test later in the chapter, but in all probability, your child is going to score relatively high in this Factor.

This is a very high score on the revenge-seeking (payback) DQ scale among children of all ages. This elevated score equates to kids and teens who tend to lash out angrily at parents and siblings for revenge. It is common for family members to avoid (or placate) this Porcupine out of fear of facing the wrath.

Our study revealed that these children and teens had often experienced some significant loss during childhood. The loss could be from a death, divorce, or even moving two or more times. This loss caused them to feel insecure and to lash out at the person(s) they subconsciously thought might have been responsible for their loss.

Children and teenagers with this elevated DQ Factor score also seemed to be defensive and self-protective as if they had been ridiculed and picked on more than normal children. Another common experience among children with this elevated score was their tendency to have a physical feature (skin color, weight, etc.) that caused them to become the center of negative attention in school and among their peers.

On the positive side, these children scored unusually high in introspective and interpersonal intelligence scales. This means they are very smart and acutely tuned in to what and how they are feeling. In short, they are highly sensitive.

---

19 to 30 (a) answers with approximately 10 (b) answers

As a precursor, it is important to keep these scores in perspective. If your child or teenager scored high in this DQ Factor, be careful not to leap to conclusions. High scores do not translate into emotional or psychological problems, nor are they an indicator of intelligence. They are merely a correlation of the type of discipline your child tends to respond to best.

A score of this elevation indicates you definitely have a child with acute Porcupine tendencies. Unlike the previous score, children and teenagers in this range tend to be less hostile and dramatic in their payback/revenge behaviors. Don't, however, make the mistake of thinking these kids are not strongly motivated to dole out the anger and punishment when they are feeling minimized, unimportant, or insignificant.

A noted characteristic of this elevation of DQ Factor #3 is that this child or teenager will hold on to anger and seek revenge for extended periods of time. We found that once hurt, this child is very slow to forgive, and it is doubtful that he will ever forget.

Although this child may not be as aggressive and manipulative in his get-even motives as is the case with higher scores, you are nonetheless likely feeling stressed and tested to the limits. In hopes of offering you a little encouragement, it is quite common for parents of children scoring at this level to feel like failures far more often than other parents. You are not.

---

9 to 18 (a) answers with approximately 13 or fewer (b) answers

This is a moderate Porcupine DQ Factor score. Oddly enough, this was the only test result range that produced an occasional false positive for DQ Factor #3. We found that about 20 percent of DQ Factor #1—Bears and about 12 percent of DQ Factor #2—Monkeys also scored elevated DQ Factor #3—Porcupine scores.

There were two reasons for this. The first is that there is definitely crossover between the Factors. The second is seen in parents who experience a high level of guilt, especially while they are taking the tests. Guilt, in parents' minds, caused them to focus more on what they had done (or had not done) for their child than on their child's misbehavior. In this case, remember the previous admonition: Try to answer these questions objectively.

Children and teens who scored in this range also tended to score in the exceptionally high range in verbal IQ skills. In an interesting combination of intelligence, they also scored in the upper 20 percent in what is called *kinesthetic intelligence*. This is a measurement of a person's coordination, fine motor skills, and often athleticism.

---

5 to 8 (a) answers with approximately 13 or fewer (b) answers

Definitely the lower end of the Porcupine DQ scale. The high (b) range score indicates you feel frustrated and probably more guilty than you should. Still, this range of score indicates some minor to moderate Porcupine characteristics, but Porcupine is likely not the predominant DQ Factor for your child.

Do not be surprised if your child or teenager scored in a similar low to moderate range in DQ Factors #1 and #2. About 26 percent of those studied did not fit an obvious (high score) DQ Factor, but instead displayed combinations of moderate scores.

Any other combination with fewer than 5 (a) answers and 10 or fewer (b) answers

Definitely not a Porcupine!

Continue to look through this section, as this DQ Factor commonly crosses over into both Monkey and Bear DQ Factors.

Note: Regardless of the number of (c) answers, they serve only to rule out this DQ Factor and do not have any special significance on their own.

THE BENNETT FAMILY

As previously mentioned, at the end of each week my staff and I would gather to discuss particularly notable families from the previous week. It was the responsibility of each intern to bring to the group one case family in each of the four DQ Factor categories: Bears, Monkeys, Porcupines, and Lambs. On this particular Saturday morning, we were introduced to the Bennett family. We all agreed that eight-year-old John Jr., despite being a revenge-seeking Porcupine, was destined to become a stand-up comic.

The Bennett family consisted of the following members:

PARENTS

Mom: Jackie

Dad: John

CHILDREN

Ruthie (10)

John Jr. (8)

Justin (4)

BACKGROUND

Since her divorce twenty-eight months ago, Jackie had been struggling to meet the rigid demands of a single mom with a full-time job. Her normal Monday through Friday routine started with getting the kids up, fed, dressed, and off to school, or, in four-year-old Justin's case, extended-day preschool.

Weekends were often just as hectic, if not more so. Because the older children had various activities ranging from soccer to Girl Scouts, Jackie met herself coming around corners. Her real estate office manager was fairly understanding, but weekends were when most couples went house-shopping, and finances being what they were, Jackie could ill afford to miss many opportunities.

Jackie's estranged husband, John, had the children on alternating weekends. By all indications, he was an involved dad and had good relationships with each of his children.

Jackie had begun dating a man she had met through her job. Thomas, employed by Jackie's company as a mortgage banker, had met her through several real estate transactions. The two hit it off and had been dating for about six weeks, and the relationship looked as though it might have a future. Thomas had two daughters of his own from a previous marriage: Victoria, who was Ruthie's age, and three-year-old Tony.

On weekends, Thomas and Jackie would bring their kids to the office, where the older daughters would enjoy time together. The two little ones seemed to play for hours in an empty office where they could pour out a mountain of toys.

But John Jr. (nicknamed J. J.) was a different story. Had Jackie been more attuned to the warning signs with her son, she would have seen trouble brewing.

SCENARIO

The following scenario took place on a Saturday morning. Jackie had to work and had mentioned to the kids that Thomas was going to stop by, and they would all go to the office together. Ruthie and Justin seemed fine with the plan, but John Jr. had other thoughts.

"I'm sick of going to the office, Mom! There's absolutely nothing for me to do. I mean, Ruthie and Victoria go to the mall and do things they want to do, and Justin and that little fat blob Tony just sit around eating Legos. I want to stay home, Mom; this is killing me!"

"J. J.," Jackie replied, "I'm sure that we can figure out something for you to do at the office. How about you doing some filing for me and Thomas and earning some extra allowance?"

"Oh, there's a treat for me!" John stated sarcastically. "I get to hang out for four hours practicing my alphabetical filing skills so that someday I can grow up to be a filing expert. And I get an extra fifty cents now! Gee, Mom, maybe you could take me to the mall later and I could buy those new shoelaces I've been wanting! Oh, wait, they cost fifty cents each. Well, maybe I can work all day today and we could go buy one, and then I'll work all day next Saturday and then we could go get the other one."

Even though Jackie clearly didn't seem to appreciate her son's sarcastic humor, we were getting quite the kick out of it.

"Well then, what do you suggest, young man? I already talked to your father, and he asked if we could trade weekends because he has something to do, and I'm not going to leave an eight-year-old home alone on a Saturday."

"Why not?" John Jr. protested. "David's parents [apparently neighbors] leave him home when they go to his grandmother's house. They don't drag him over there because they know there isn't anything for David to do all day— unless you call watching his grandmother's teeth sit in a glass of water fun!"

As guilt settled into Jackie's mind, she began to soften on her position. "I'll make you a deal. We'll try it this one time if I can find someone for you to spend the day with—either David's parents or Michael's. But I warn you, if none of them can watch you, then you are going to go with me to the office."

"That's cool, Mom. I'll call David and see if I can hang with him today."

A few minutes later, our recorded transcripts reveal that John Jr. had received permission from David's parents to spend the day with their family. This was the end of the morning tape. We picked up the conversation at 5:02 P.M. that same afternoon as Jackie and the two girls came home from the office.

"John, are you home?" Jackie called out from the kitchen.

"Yeah," came the loud reply from down the hallway as John sauntered into the kitchen where Jackie and the girls were putting groceries away.

"Did you have a good day with David?" she inquired.

"David's a moron! I sent him home at 1:00," John replied.

"You know I do not want to hear you talking that way, young man. And what do you mean, you sent him home at 1:00? You were supposed to be spending the day together. That was the deal David's parents and I made. What did they say about his coming home?"

Hesitating for a moment, John Jr. replied, "David's dad called and asked me if I wanted to come over. Then I guess his grandmother called and she fell, and they all rushed over to her house. Besides, I don't need a baby-sitter. I told David to go home when he started acting all big-shot."

"Oh, my! Is his grandmother okay? I need to call Marnie right away and ask how she is doing. We'll talk about your disobeying orders when I get off the phone, young man."

(Note to reader: At this point it is only fair to warn you that neither my team nor I condone bad language and hostilities between siblings. The following dialogue between John Jr. and Justin has been edited to be less offensive, but I think you'll get the meaning.)

In a low, mocking tone of voice we overheard John saying, "We'll talk about your disobeying orders when I get off the phone, young man.' Ooooohhhhh . . . . I'm gonna wet my pants I'm soooooooo scared."

Of course, then the youngest child, Justin, overheard the smart remarks and shouted, "Mommmmmmmyyyyyy! J. J. is talking back. He said he was going to wet his pants!"

"Shut up, you little toad!" John Jr. commanded in a subdued yet very hostile tone. "Have you ever had a Lego stuck so far up your nose they have to take you to the hospital to get it out with scissors and pliers?"

"No," came a sheepish reply.

"Well, I'm gonna cram so many Legos up your nose that a whole team of doctors and nurses are going to think that's the only place you play with 'em."

"Shut up, J. J."

"You shut up, toad!"

"I'm telling Mom."

"Go ahead and tell her. . . . See what I care, you little blob."

"Mom! J. J. called me a blob and he's . . ."

"*Shut up,*" John Jr. said in a half-hearted pleading tone. "Look, I'll give you my Magic Eight Ball if you just drop it."

"Okay!" came the reply without a moment of hesitation. "I'm going to get it before you change your mind."

With that said, we heard the younger brother shuffling out of the room, followed by this muted comment by John Jr.: "Dumb bunny . . . that stupid Eight Ball hasn't worked since the day after Christmas."

We pick up the conversation approximately ten minutes later as Jackie calls John Jr. into the kitchen.

In a stern but subdued tone of voice, we overheard Jackie ask, "Do you have something you want to tell me, J. J.?"

"About what?"

"About a certain scratch on Tom's car that your friend David says wasn't an accident."

After about fifteen seconds of silence, Jackie spoke again.

"Look, J. J., David already told his father what happened to the car and that you did it on purpose because you don't like Tom. He also told me that when he said he was going to tell his parents, you got angry and sent him home. Isn't that about what happened?"

"I didn't do it on purpose. We were just riding our bikes in the driveway, and I lost control and got too close to Mr. Timmons's car. He shouldn't have left it in *our* driveway anyway. He doesn't live here!"

"I want you to go to your room right now while I call Tom and ask him to check his car to see how much damage you did to it. I don't even want to look at you right now. You go to your room, and I'll call you when I'm ready to talk."

Jackie later related to us that as she sat alone at the kitchen table to gather her thoughts, she replayed in her head the conversation she had with J. J. *He shouldn't have left his car in our driveway because he doesn't live here.* Then she recalled the earlier conversation where she mentioned that her ex was not able to watch J. J. today because he had something else going on.

After a few moments spent gathering her thoughts, Jackie began to piece the events of the day together. She soon realized that J. J. had impulsively acted out his anger and frustration at both her and his father over the divorce, and days like today were a constant reminder of how difficult post-divorce life can be at times.

She correctly surmised that Tom, undeserving as he was, had become the focal point of J. J.'s anger. J. J. had driven his bicycle past Tom's car, which was parked in his father's spot in the driveway one too many times. With each pass, J. J. was reminded that his parents were not together and that another man was in his father's place. J. J.'s subconscious thoughts were to punish Tom for taking his father's place. His juvenile way of processing information also convinced him that by scratching Tom's car, he would be getting back at his mom, who seemed to be replacing his dad with this stranger.

We listened intently and were very impressed with the way Jackie got past her own angry thoughts and was able to address her son's underlying motive for revenge when she called him back.

"I know you think Tom is taking your dad's place in the family, J. J.," she said softly. "I can assure you that he is not ever going to replace your father. Your dad will always be your dad, and even though the two of us will never get back together, it doesn't mean that we don't love you just as much."

Pausing for a moment, she continued, "I also know that you saw an opportunity to hurt Tom, and maybe even send him a message, by scratching his car. I understand how you could have thought those things, but you did the wrong thing. Do you understand what I am saying, honey?"

Speaking for the first time since sitting down at the kitchen table, John Jr. replied, "I'm sorry, Mom. I don't know why I did it. I was just riding my bike by, and the thought came into my brain, and I didn't think about it any more. I just scratched his car. What should I do?"

In a soft and very warm tone, Jackie replied, "I think you should call Tom and tell him you are sorry and that you will make it up to him by doing enough chores to pay to get the scratch taken out."

"All right. I can do that. But I'm not going to play with that narc, David, anymore."

Summary

J. J.'s misbehavior was a classic example of how DQ #3—Porcupines reason through things. It isn't that they wake up in the morning with revenge, payback, getting even, ill will, malevolence, repayment, retribution, ruthlessness, and vindictiveness on their minds. They are often driven by subconscious thoughts.

In J. J.'s case, he had taken the usual dose of emotional hits when his parents divorced. Divorce can make many children feel as though they are insignificant and even unimportant. Because children don't possess the skills that come with maturity to talk through these feelings, the feelings end up coming out in other ways. J. J.'s revenge motive actually produced the desired effect while he was engaged in the act of scratching Tom's car. At that moment he felt powerful, important, and significant in that he was able to cause damage and thus instill grief in the person who was responsible for hurting him—Tom. It was a bonus that his mom would also experience some pain when Tom told her that his car was scratched while in the family's driveway. J. J. had not thought past his desire to punish and what would eventually happen when the adults found out it was he who scratched the car. Even if he did think far enough down the road to realize that he would receive the blame, he would just claim it was an accident.

Jackie handled the situation with poise and intelligence. She picked up on his hurt feelings and misguided desire for revenge. She even did well when assigning the punishment of doing chores *for Tom* and not for her or others. By assigning J. J. to do chores for Tom, she followed the path of *logical consequences*. Sure, he could make money and pay for the damage in any number of ways, but by connecting his misbehavior to the person he hurt, she was forcing J. J. to engage Tom and therefore confront his feelings.

We all agreed that Jackie should merit our Parent of the Week award. Cheap as it may be, we had anonymously set up a program where we sent McDonald's gift certificates to certain parents or children who did or said something extraordinary and were deserving of something fun and special. Since we didn't reveal until later who the free food coupons were from, it was always fun to listen in when the surprise arrived.

Are You Living with a Porcupine?

Now it is time to see if you are living with a Porcupine. The essential questions below were extracted from the complete DQ Factor battery of tests. Over a period of time, we found that these questions were more than sufficient to fully flush out a child's DQ Factor.

As you did with the previous test, try your best to separate yourself from any emotional investment in the answers or outcome. You can best do this by imagining you are an outsider, but one who knows your child inside and out, and you have been asked to evaluate him or her.

Read the following questions carefully. Each has been designed to correspond to any age child or teenager. Answer the questions below by circling

(a) if you *strongly agree* with the statement,

(b) if you *somewhat agree* with the statement, or

(c) if you *do not agree* with the statement.

DQ Factor #3—Porcupine Test

1. S/he seems to get her/his way far more often than the other children.
   Circle one: (a) (b) (c)

2. Even though I think a cooling-off period is called for, s/he keeps badgering me.
   Circle one: (a) (b) (c)

3. S/he tends to be somewhat on the perfectionistic side when it comes to certain things.
   Circle one: (a) (b) (c)

4. I would say s/he is slightly less happy than other children or teenagers her/his age.
   Circle one: (a) (b) (c)

5. I would have to say that s/he has her/his own agenda going on inside her/his mind.
   Circle one: (a) (b) (c)

6. S/he seems to care about winning more than most children or teenagers.
   Circle one: (a) (b) (c)

7. Whether it is a board game or an argument, s/he hates to lose.
   Circle one: (a) (b) (c)

8. S/he covers emotions well and won't often let anyone know that her/his feelings have been hurt.
   Circle one: (a) (b) (c)

9. S/he is slow to cool down after an argument.
   Circle one: (a) (b) (c)

10. Sometimes s/he will hold on to anger longer than I can imagine.
    Circle one: (a) (b) (c)

11. After s/he has her/his feelings hurt, you can bet that there will be some retaliation coming.
Circle one: (a)   (b)   (c)

12. S/he seems to obsess (talking and thinking) about people who have hurt her/his feelings.
Circle one: (a)   (b)   (c)

13. I can think something is completely done and over with and then she/he will bring it up days or even weeks later.
Circle one: (a)   (b)   (c)

14. S/he lies fairly convincingly.
Circle one: (a)   (b)   (c)

15. Unless I confront her/him with hard evidence, s/he is likely not to admit fault.
Circle one: (a)   (b)   (c)

16. S/he is stoic and seems unemotional in situations where s/he should be full of emotion.
Circle one: (a)   (b)   (c)

17. S/he learned to walk either earlier than normal or on schedule.
Circle one: (a)   (b)   (c)

18. S/he occasionally does or says mean or violent things that worry me.
Circle one: (a)   (b)   (c)

19. S/he seems to enjoy action stories over other types of stories.
Circle one: (a)   (b)   (c)

20. S/he has a quick temper.
Circle one: (a)   (b)   (c)

21. S/he tends to want sympathy from me whenever anything bad happens to her/him.
Circle one: (a)   (b)   (c)

22. In school, s/he is more prone to taking shortcuts in order to get the work done quickly than to getting it done right.
    Circle one: (a)   (b)   (c)

23. Sometimes I wonder if s/he sets goals too low because of a fear of failure.
    Circle one: (a)   (b)   (c)

24. S/he can be rather hotheaded when crossed.
    Circle one: (a)   (b)   (c)

25. I would say that telling little white lies doesn't seem to bother her/him.
    Circle one: (a)   (b)   (c)

26. S/he doesn't prepare well for tests in school.
    Circle one: (a)   (b)   (c)

27. S/he is more opinionated than most kids her/his own age.
    Circle one: (a)   (b)   (c)

28. If given the chance and s/he doesn't want to do it, s/he will try to get out of doing what I have told her/him to do.
    Circle one: (a)   (b)   (c)

29. I think s/he is more prone to taking the shortcut to getting things done.
    Circle one: (a)   (b)   (c)

30. S/he wants to be noticed when doing things like sports or school plays rather than taking a behind-the-scenes role.
    Circle one: (a)   (b)   (c)

31. For his/her age, my child is a natural organizer.
    Circle one: (a)   (b)   (c)

32. I sometimes wonder that s/he suffers from low self-esteem.
    Circle one: (a)   (b)   (c)

33. If standing in line, s/he is the kind of person who would say something to the other people rather than look the other way.
Circle one: (a)   (b)   (c)

34. I've heard her/him get so angry that s/he shouts at people.
Circle one: (a)   (b)   (c)

35. S/he tends to see rules in shades of gray rather than rules being black and white.
Circle one: (a)   (b)   (c)

36. S/he seems to thrive on excitement.
Circle one: (a)   (b)   (c)

37. S/he will tend to leave for tomorrow what should have been taken care of today.
Circle one: (a)   (b)   (c)

38. S/he will do things like draw in books even though s/he knows it is not right.
Circle one: (a)   (b)   (c)

39. S/he was toilet trained either earlier than normal or on schedule.
Circle one: (a)   (b)   (c)

40. I think s/he has little regard for other people's property.
Circle one: (a)   (b)   (c)

41. It wouldn't shock me to find that s/he could be mean or cruel to an animal or insect.
Circle one: (a)   (b)   (c)

42. When doing homework, s/he has difficulty concentrating if there are too many distractions in the room.
Circle one: (a)   (b)   (c)

43. For his/her age, my child is very persuasive.
Circle one: (a)   (b)   (c)

44. I wish I could get him/her to think before speaking.
    Circle one: (a)   (b)   (c)

---

45. S/he bores easily and needs stimulus.
    Circle one: (a)   (b)   (c)

---

46. I think s/he believes that winning is more important than just playing the game.
    Circle one: (a)   (b)   (c)

---

47. S/he tends to be more at ease with kids/teenagers who are more quiet and timid.
    Circle one: (a)   (b)   (c)

---

48. To my knowledge, s/he is not particularly afraid of the dark.
    Circle one: (a)   (b)   (c)

---

49. I think s/he would hurt the feelings of others to get what s/he wants.
    Circle one: (a)   (b)   (c)

---

50. S/he has a rigid way of seeing things and doesn't try to see it from the others' point of view.
    Circle one: (a)   (b)   (c)

---

51. S/he discounts other people's feelings as not as important as hers/his.
    Circle one: (a)   (b)   (c)

---

52. S/he doesn't like taking orders and makes It plain.
    Circle one: (a)   (b)   (c)

---

53. S/he will argue just for the sake of arguing.
    Circle one: (a)   (b)   (c)

---

54. I think s/he doesn't particularly get along well with people who come across as bossy and authoritative.
    Circle one: (a)   (b)   (c)

---

55. My child/teenager is very good at making up excuses for why s/he did something the wrong way.
Circle one: (a)   (b)   (c)

56. I would not characterize my child as being mild-tempered.
Circle one: (a)   (b)   (c)

57. My child is more apt to stick to her/his guns than to be talked out of something.
Circle one: (a)   (b)   (c)

58. S/he is more assertive than passive.
Circle one: (a)   (b)   (c)

59. S/he loses her/his temper more than most people that age.
Circle one: (a)   (b)   (c)

60. S/he would likely agree with someone just to avoid a confrontation.
Circle one: (a)   (b)   (c)

61. S/he was talking either earlier than normal or on schedule.
Circle one: (a)   (b)   (c)

62. S/he has a better-than-average vocabulary and is not afraid to use it.
Circle one: (a)   (b)   (c)

SCORING YOUR DQ FACTOR #3—PORCUPINE TEST

Add up the number of (a) answers and put the number here: _____

Add up the number of (b) answers and put the number here: _____

Add up the number of (c) answers and put the number here: _____

Interpreting Your Child's/Teenager's DQ #3 Test

Total number of questions   62

47 or more (a) answers with approximately 15 (b) answers

No question about it, your child or teenager fits a DQ Factor #3 profile. This is especially true if this elevated score is found in conjunction with a high FED-UP (parent feelings quiz) score from earlier in the chapter.

To reiterate, this is a very high score on the revenge-seeking (payback) DQ scale among children of all ages. This elevated score equates to kids and teens who tend to lash out angrily at parents and siblings for revenge. It is common for family members to avoid (or placate) this Porcupine out of fear of facing his or her wrath.

Our study revealed that these children and teens had often experienced some significant loss during childhood. The loss could be from a death, divorce, or even moving two or more times. This loss caused them to feel insecure and to lash out at the person(s) they subconsciously believe might have been responsible for their loss.

Children and teenagers with this elevated DQ Factor score also seemed to be defensive and self-protective, as if they had been ridiculed and picked on more than normal children. Another common experience among children with this elevated score was their tendency to have a physical feature (weight, skin color, etc.) that caused them to become the center of negative attention in school and among their peers.

On the positive side, these children scored abnormally high in introspective and interpersonal intelligence scales. This means they are very smart and acutely tuned in to what and how they are feeling. In short, they are highly sensitive.

30 to 46 (a) answers with approximately 10 (b) answers

Scores at this level indicate you definitely have a Porcupine on your hands.

Unlike the extremely high score above, kids and teens in this range tend to be less agitated (less on a mission) in their desire to find revenge and pay you back for causing them to feel insecure, minimized, unloved, or insignificant. As an aside, the event(s) leading up to the Porcupine feeling this way are probably fairly obvious—you just need to look at it from his or her perspective to find out what transpired.

This child or teenager will hold on to anger and revenge motives for a long time if necessary. We found that once hurt, this child is very slow to forgive, and it is doubtful that he will ever forget.

Although this child may not be as aggressive and controlling as one with higher scores, you are likely feeling stressed and tested to the limits. It is also common for parents at this level in the DQ #3 evaluation to feel like they are unappreciated or complete failures. You may find yourself saying things such as, "I can't believe he would treat me that way after all the things I've done for him."

---

18 to 30 (a) answers with approximately 17 or fewer (b) answers

This is a moderate Porcupine DQ Factor score.

Oddly enough, this was the only test result range that could (although infrequently) produce a false positive for DQ Factor #3. We found that the score could fluctuate as much as 20 percent based on how guilty a parent was feeling at the time she or he took the test. Therefore, if you are the type of parent who often feels inadequate or guilty, it is possible that you scored higher in this area than you should have. If you think this is the case, you may want your spouse or someone else who knows you and your child well to take this one particular test for you.

Children and teens who scored in this range tended to score in the exceptionally high range in verbal IQ skills. As a unique skill combination, they also tended to score in the upper 20 percentile in what is called *kinesthetic intelligence*. This means they are good with their hands and exceptionally well coordinated.

---

10 to 17 (a) answers with approximately 18 or fewer (b) answers

Definitely the lower end of the Porcupine DQ scale. The high (b) range score indicates you feel frustrated and probably more guilty than you should. Still, this range of score indicates some minor to moderate Porcupine characteristics, which would fall more toward holding on to anger for a long time than seeking active revenge.

It is very possible that a score at this level means your child displays a mixture of DQ Factors #1 and #2. We found approximately 26 percent of the children and teenagers who scored moderately high on this DQ Factor also scored moderately high on DQ Factors #1 and #2. If this is the case, you should not be alarmed at all. In fact, we found this combination to be a surprisingly resilient individual. We also found that these children and teenagers had experienced significant losses (divorce, death, separation, moving, etc.) within the past three to five years, but were on their way out of the emotional pain.

Finally, it was not at all unusual to find a DQ Bear dominant Factor (high score) with a DQ Porcupine (medium score) as a secondary Factor.

Any other combination with fewer than 5 (a) answers and 10 or fewer (b) answers

Definitely not a Porcupine!

Continue to look through this section, as this DQ Factor commonly crosses over into both Monkey and Bear DQ Factors.

Note: Regardless of the number of (c) answers, they serve only to rule out this DQ Factor and do not have any special significance on their own.

THE DQ RX FOR PORCUPINES

As previously stated, there is a lengthy continuum of disciplinary techniques available to parents when their child has broken a rule and stepped over a boundary. One of the primary objectives of the DQ study was to focus on and identify both the ineffective and effective disciplinary techniques used with specific DQ Factors. My team and I found it remarkable that the majority of parents repeatedly utilized nearly identical methods of discipline—even when that discipline proved to be ineffective.

The list below comprises the most frequent disciplinary methods used by parents of Porcupines. The list is separated by type of discipline and effectiveness. In this situation, effectiveness refers to both an objective and subjective percentage we assigned to each discipline form as we witnessed its implementation and overall success rate in creating behavioral changes among DQ Factor #3—Porcupines.

Type of Discipline with DQ Factor #3—Porcupines	Effectiveness
AGGRESSIVE SPANKING This term refers to any spanking technique that ranged from taking the child's pants	12 PERCENT

down and spanking with an open palm, to utilizing a spanking instrument such as a wooden spoon.

We found that strong spankings were largely ineffective discipline techniques with a Porcupine because of the anger-revenge cycle that it produced. Typically, our DQ Factor Porcupine angrily mis-behaved in an attempt to punish a parent for some perceived injustice that sent ripples through his self-esteem and significance. If the parent responds in anger and retaliation, then again we have a serious cycle of anger—revenge—anger to manage.

Because strong spankings are often received as personally demeaning and hurtful by most children, let alone Porcupines, we found this to be one of the least effective forms of punishment.

Note: There were no abuse issues throughout the study. Societal standards still view spanking with objects that do not leave permanent marks to be acceptable. For the record, I am not opposed to spanking, but I am opposed to using any instrument (spoons, hangers, belts, etc.) to spank children. Utilizing these items depersonalizes the discipline process and can clearly inflict excessive and unintentional injury.

SIMPLE SWATTING   22 PERCENT

This term refers to a spanking technique that would be called a simple swat (or series of swats) to the child's buttocks, delivered by the hand to the outside of the pants and/or underwear.

Simple swatting was slightly more effective than its more aggressive counterpart, but we still found this to be one of the least effective methods along the discipline continuum.

IGNORING   20 PERCENT

Whereas ignoring was an effective disciplinary tool with both DQ Factor Bears and Monkeys, it is not an effective tool with Porcupines.

Ignoring is the premeditated practice of not letting your child's misbehaviors get to you. Parents who practice this effectively will act as though the misbehavior was not even noticed or, at the most, no big deal. When parents used this approach with our Porcupines, these children and teenagers perceived that to be an even greater affront to their self-worth. When this occurred, they often increased their revenge tactics.

Remember, when this DQ Factor retaliates, it is done to elevate his or her self-esteem by commanding your attention and respect. Ignoring his efforts at gaining attention and significance served to frustrate our Porcupine, thus prolonging the inevitable outburst.

VERBAL REPRIMANDS   47 PERCENT

This form of discipline worked more effectively with DQ Factor Porcupines than it did with DQ Factor Monkeys for a number of reasons.

Primarily, though, it was because the verbal reprimand at least acknowledged that the revenge-seeking misbehavior was received. To that degree, we found that this punishment was roughly 50/50 effective from the standpoint that it defused a portion of the Porcupine's desired outcome—acknowledgment.

TIME-OUTS   21 PERCENT

Porcupine DQ Factor types, in contrast to their Bear and Monkey counterparts, are far less social creatures. Think about it. When was the last time you saw a stuffed porcupine in the toy store?

Because they are not particularly motivated by social things, removing a Porcupine from outside stimulus (through time-outs) to go to his room proved ineffective. In our study, it was common for a Porcupine to be sent to his room for a fifteen-minute time-out, only to come out in a half-hour on his own showing no signs of remorse.

TIME-OUTS WITH EXPLANATION   41 PERCENT

One of the things we noticed was that a time-out, coupled with an acknowledgment and an explanation for the discipline, was considerably more effective than sending the Porcupine to his or her room without an explanation.

RESTRICTIONS   19 PERCENT

You may be wondering why restrictions produced such poor results with Porcupine DQ Factors when they worked so much better with the other types. You can sum it up by projecting what goes on in the mind of a persecuted, victim-thinking person when he spends hour upon hour alone with his thoughts. That's right, his victimhood is reinforced, and he becomes even more intent on seeking revenge.

The bottom line is that the way to get Porcupines to comply is to engage them, not to disengage them through isolation.

TAKING AWAY PRIVILEGES

54 PERCENT

Taking away privileges such as TV, stereo, bike proved to be a slightly less effective disciplinary action with Porcupines than with Monkeys.

We found that taking away privileges led to an interesting challenge. Each time the parent would take something away, the Porcupine would pass it off as something that didn't really matter to him. Whether it was television, skates, toys, stereos—it didn't matter because it was something he didn't want anyway.

BELITTLING

NEGATIVE IMPACT

This technique was even more ineffective with Porcupines than it was with other DQ Factors. This was because of the tentative nature of the Porcupine's self-esteem and his propensity for seeking revenge.

If you set out to choose the one action that would further destroy your Porcupine's sense of emotional security and well-being, belittling would definitely be your first choice. This form of discipline is destined to lead to increased immediate conduct problems, as well as more serious future conflicts.

THREATS   16 PERCENT

As the proud parent of a Porcupine, you've
got to know that anger is perhaps the worst
emotion to interject into your child's discipline.
Whenever a Porcupine senses discipline coming
from anger, he will meet your anger with his own,
which is fueled by revenge.

As was the case with the previous DQ Factors,
we found that most parents (72 percent) did
not follow through with the threat or promised
consequence. This scenario caused the children
to disregard not only present and future threats,
but legitimate requests.

Keep in mind that a boundary is only a
request if it does not have a communicated,
understood, and fully anticipated potential
for consequences.

NATURAL CONSEQUENCES   76 PERCENT

Natural consequences worked very
effectively with Porcupine DQ Factors
because they are not received in a cruel
or personal fashion. As with all DQ Factors,
natural consequences produce positive
results because they are based on how
God and the universe function. The Bible is
very clear in presenting God's laws of sowing
and reaping. He states the rules upfront (in
black and white) that we are free to choose
any course we desire, but there are natural
consequences (both positive and negative)
to our choices. The sooner we can transform
our children's decision-making skills to the
point where they weigh options and
consequences, the better.

The DQ Rx

In addition to the insights gained by examining the aforementioned typical types of discipline used in conjunction with DQ Factor Porcupines, our research also produced some other effective boundary and discipline techniques. We found the following actions and ideas to be powerful in neutralizing the revenge-driven misbehaving characteristics of Porcupines.

Rx #1

Natural Consequences

Whenever possible, go with natural consequences with your DQ Factor Porcupine. As an example, my teenage son has the chore of emptying the trash into the barrels for pickup each Wednesday. I'm sure none of you reading this can associate with what I'm about to say, but he had a tendency to forget. (Go ahead and collect yourselves. . . . I'll wait.) Some weeks he would remember, but others required my wife or me doing his chore for him.

On a Thursday morning after missing the trash collection, and as a natural consequence of his forgetfulness, I asked a favor of him. In an extremely calm fashion, I asked him if he had any suggestions as to how we should handle the fact that our trash containers were overflowing in each room and that we had missed the trash pickup day. Like any normal teenage boy, he stared quizzically at me, sort of like my golden retriever looks when he can't figure out what I'm saying. In short, my son had no recommendation for dealing with the trash situation.

Putting a little acting enthusiasm behind my voice, I exclaimed, "I know what will work! Why don't you do me a huge favor and take the full trash bags from each room, put them in your car, and take them to a dumpster?" The look alone from him was priceless.

Again, I did so without the faintest hint of anger or punishment for his forgetfulness. I'm sure he thought I was one fry short of a Happy Meal, but he shrugged his shoulders and did as he was asked.

A car is naturally a teenage boy's pride and joy, and putting stinky garbage bags in his car was not my son's idea of a day at Disneyland. I'll tell you what, though: He never forgot to take the trash out again. Natural consequences—I highly endorse their use.

Rx #2
INVOLUNTARY DISCLOSURE

They aren't precisely what I would term disciplinary techniques, but there are several interrogation methods that I first discovered as a police officer (no bright lights, bamboo shoots, or rubber hoses) and later found most helpful with my patients as well as my kids. I began referring to this technique as *involuntary disclosure*, as it represents nonverbal cues that detect another's thoughts or emotions. The reason these cues are so helpful is that getting at the emotional truth behind actions, such as our child's misbehavior, can be guarded by the subconscious and therefore invisible to the individual. Or, the child may simply not want to reveal the real reason he chose to act out. Either way, involuntary disclosure will help you learn the DQ Factor motive (control, attention, revenge, or defeatist mind-set) behind your child's misbehavior.

The interviewing techniques involve asking specific questions and then looking for subtle changes. Here are the things to look for anytime you ask a sensitive question of someone and they either don't consciously know, or do not want *you* to know, the truth.

Change in facial expression
Look for the eyebrows to move up and for the mouth to adjust as though

the individual is biting his lip. This is an indication that the person is uncomfortable with a question (it's hitting close to home) or he is lying.

Face flushing

Embarrassment and guilt register the same emotions in the central nervous system. If the person flushes red as though embarrassed, you are on to a sensitive area or he is lying.

Diverting eye contact

When we lie to someone, we automatically divert eye contact. This is called a *shame-based response*. Whenever you are talking to your children, look them square in the eyes. When they tell you a lie (or half truth), they will look away momentarily or, in some cases, longer.

Involuntary shifting

Kids and teenagers will nearly always shift their weight from one foot to another or from side to side when they are uncomfortable about a question. Take note of such movements, as it means you are on the right track with your probing questions or he is lying.

Involuntary smiling

It's amazing, but children and teenagers will involuntarily smile or laugh when you ask a question that scores a direct hit. For instance, if you were to ask your child why he carved his name into the windowsill, he will likely reply, "I don't know." If you ask him if he did it to get back at you for not letting him have that pocket knife he wanted, you are likely to see an involuntary smile or nervous laugh.

The Vegas nerve

No, this is not the mechanism that enables gamblers to place large bets. This is the technical name for the large nerve that runs vertically through the temple and down the neck. When an individual is either subconsciously covering up information or lying outright, this nerve will twitch, caused by an increase in respiration and subsequent blood pressure. You have to look carefully to spot this one, but it is a can't-miss truth detector.

Rx #3

SELF-RESTRAINT

It's no secret that it's difficult to practice self-restraint when your child has just lashed out at you in a revenge-laced effort to hurt your feelings. "I hate you!" or "I want to go live with Dad!" are just a sampling of the things we heard from Porcupines to their parents. As tough as this is, you need to avoid being drawn into an angry exchange cycle of paying him back for hurting you by saying something equally hurtful. Porcupine DQ Factors react to *your* angry reaction by feeling justified in seeking revenge. Once the revenge—anger—revenge cycle starts between you and your child, you may have the last word, but you will never win.

Rx #4

STAY ON THE SUBJECT

Winning seems to be the goal of both parent and child throughout the discipline process. Each of us has a point to make and we want the other to acknowledge it. Your child misbehaved because of *this reason* and *that reason*. You want him to stop it and to admit wrongdoing so you do and say *these things*.

Most parents and children (especially Porcupines and Monkeys) get so caught up in trying to win that the original misbehavior is forgotten and the conflict becomes all about winning. The will to win and to prove the other wrong takes on a life of its own.

As stated above, you can believe you have won the argument by getting the last word in ("I don't want to hear another word out of you"), but the victory is short-lived. There is strength in being self-controlled, listening, responding, and then allowing your child to have the final word. Do not allow yourself or your Porcupine to stray from the point. Gently return yourselves to the reason for the discussion by stating, "Let's get back to the point of this conversation. We were talking about . . . "

Rx #5
EMPATHETIC LISTENING

Help me to understand are perhaps the four most powerful words in the English language when it comes to connecting with your kids, especially with the Porcupine DQ Factor. I've often used this technique even when I fully understood what and why one of my kids did what they did. Making this reflective statement—"Help me to understand why you are feeling this way"—communicates your care, concern, and desire to see the issue from his perspective. This is very strong medicine.

Rx #6
REFLECTIVE LISTENING

Equally strong medicine, especially with Porcupines, is a technique called *reflective listening*. This wonderful technique simply requires you to listen to your child's point and then echo it back to him, preceded by: "So what you are saying is . . ." or "So if I am hearing you correctly, you are saying . . ."

This technique allows two wonderful things. First, it communicates to your child that you are listening, and second, it allows him to hear his point from outside of his own brain. You might be shocked how odd our perspectives sound when we hear them from someone else.

Rx #7

DEFERRED BLAME

One of my favorite techniques with all DQ Factors, but especially with Porcupines, is called *deferred blame*. Our kids (adults as well) will avoid taking responsibility for misbehaving. It is always someone else's fault that they had to do what they did. Therefore, deferred blame is the technique that calmly and tactically removes you from the blame game and forces them to look at owning the problem they caused.

This is accomplished by following a simple rule. Whenever you are talking about the consequence (discipline) for your child's misbehaving, you must precede it with, "I'm sorry you chose to do X." You don't have to say why you are sorry, because the power in this statement comes from his hearing that you are sorry that HE CHOSE to do it. By framing his misbehavior in terms of HIS CHOICE, he is forced to own it instead of to assign blame.

Rx #8

PUTTING YOUR PORCUPINE TO WORK (THE DECK OF CHORES)

Shock! What worked well with Bears and Monkeys was found to be equally effective with Porcupines.

The Deck of Chores employs between ten and fifty blank four-by-six cards. On each card write a different chore on one side and the card number on the reverse. Make sure you write age-appropriate chores for your child so you do not have your five-year-old up in the oak tree with a chainsaw.

When your child misbehaves and it is time to decide on his discipline, we found that a visit to The Deck of Chores was both entertaining and effective, but it did something for each DQ Factor that we had not anticipated. Because the child was the one to select a discipline chore from the deck, he could not really blame the parent for making him do something he hated to do. After all, it wasn't his parent's choice of chores, but his alone.

A Final View of the Porcupine Zoo

As you and I examine the various animals in the DQ zoo, I can't help but wonder if you are being consumed with anxiety. I fret that you may be pulling your hair out because you have identified that not only are you the curator of the Porcupine habitat, but that your child seems to be the poster child for Porcupines all over the world.

I must reinforce that Porcupine DQ Factors are not sick, tortured, demented, wild-eyed nocturnal children who live to punish you. They are wonderful, bright, and amazing kids who are dealing with their hurts and emotions in the best way they know how. As ineffective as these coping mechanisms have proven to be, they just don't know another way. It is up to you to help them to find new, effective ones.

There is nothing wrong with your child, nor should you run right out and purchase tranquilizer darts if he or she scored high (or even off the charts) in this DQ Factor. A high DQ Factor #3 score merely points to the underlying misbehaving motivations of your child. Knowing what drives misbehavior is the first amazing step in addressing it in the most effective manner.

CHAPTER 9

DQ Factor #4—Lambs
(The Defeatists in the Zoo)

I was looking through an old photo album of a time my wife and I took our kids to the zoo. We have photos of them in front of the bear habitat, the monkey menagerie, and even the porcupine enclosure. They were probably six and seven years old at the time, and I'm sure they enjoyed themselves. I could tell because of their broad smiles in each of the pictures.

In one photo they were holding their $12.98 each Zoo Meals (cheese sandwich, crocodile cookie, and a plastic moose). In another picture they were holding their $9.00 souvenir rabbit's foot keychains. And in another shot, my kids were wearing their $26.00 *Save the Gorilla* T-shirts for which I'm sure $20.00 goes to some unidentified rain forest in Pasadena, California. (To keep on the good side of the IRS, they probably do give two cents to some save-the-rain-forest group who taught a gorilla to lick thank-you-card envelopes. Unless you are a parent, you probably can't relate to the hold-on-to-your-wallet shakedown experience at the zoo. But the animals are fun!)

Then I came across a pleasant series of pictures that seemed to encapsulate our fourth and final DQ Factor #4—Lambs. The pictures were taken in the petting zoo. This is the small, smelly corner of the zoo where the more timid and mild-mannered animals (I refer to them as death row inmates) roam inside an enclosure. The petting zoo must be the animal kingdom equivalent of doing hard time. No television, just rude miniature visitors who poke at you, try to jump on your back, and then throw handfuls of green pellets in your face like they are some sort of animal delicacy.

Lest you think I have digressed to the point of loose associations, let me tell you where I am going with my analogy. If you check every petting zoo in the world, you will find one animal that hides in the corner trying to become invisible. You guessed it—the lamb. While the miniature goats are eating the green pellets like they are caviar, and the geese are hoping to get one good arm bite in before the alarm sounds, the poor lamb is huddled in the corner, praying for closing time. Anything! Just please make these kids go away so the lamb can get back to being the timid recluse of the zoo.

Of the four DQ Factors discovered in the survey, none tapped into our sympathies like DQ Factor #4—Lambs. In fact, when our research team got together to debrief after the study was complete, we agreed that Lambs were undoubtedly the sweetest, yet most emotionally challenging, of all of the DQ Factors. This is because they are really the *anti-*DQ Factor. By this I mean that they are nearly the reverse of each of the three previous DQ Factors. They are as timid as Bears are aggressive, as insecure as Monkeys are demanding, and as passive as Porcupines are revenge-seeking. For lack of a better or more clinical definition, our team agreed that Lambs are best described as the child you just want to hug until everything gets better.

As a DQ Factor, Lambs are the defeatists in the zoo. They tend to see themselves as weak, incapable, and destined to fail. Therefore, Lambs avoid tough and demanding situations where their successes and failures can be seen. They accomplish this through a number of avoidance techniques, but the two most common are to shrink into the background or to appear so helpless that you will do things for them.

Lambs are no different than the other three DQ Factors in that they desire and are driven to find significance, love, and importance. Whereas Bears receive significance through challenge, Monkeys through attention, and Porcupines through revenge, Lambs derive significance through perceived weakness, which causes others to come to their rescue. As an odd turnaround in motivation, we also saw that some Lamb DQ Factors achieved feelings of significance when no demands were made of them. It was as though their projected weaknesses had succeeded to the point where others didn't bother asking them to do anything. Just by being left alone, they felt significant.

Let me give you an example. After finishing a counseling session, I received a call from a young father who had heard me talking about discipline on a radio program. Bless his heart, he was calling in hopes of getting some advice to take home to his wife, who was struggling with a three-year-old and a one-year-old. He told me, "Our three-year-old daughter, Chelsea, is acting more like a baby than our one-year-old."

"Can you give me an example of what Chelsea is doing?" I inquired.

"I can give you a thousand examples, but I'll give you the one that my wife told me about last night. Chelsea goes to preschool, and up to about a month ago she was really easy to handle. She wasn't perfect, but she would try. She got herself dressed, and she would do helpful little things like get the baby's diapers and simple stuff like that. We don't know what has come over her, but she can't do anything any more. My wife has to dress her, wipe her bottom after she goes potty, and change her clothes for her. It's like she suddenly forgot how to do all the things she used to be able to do." Pausing for a moment, the young dad asked, "Is it possible for children to have small strokes where they lose their memories like old people do?"

I replied, "No, children *give* small strokes, they don't get them," apparently amusing myself somewhat more than this dad. "Here's what I think happened; you can tell me if it makes sense. Let's start with when you and your wife first started noticing your daughter's sudden inability to take care of and do things for herself."

"About five weeks ago," he replied.

"Okay, now tell me about the developmental milestones your youngest— assuming your youngest is also a girl—reached about five weeks ago."

Thinking for a few moments, he replied, "If by milestones you mean walking and talking, I can remember two pretty big events that went on at about that time. Katie started walking, and she actually started saying 'Mama.' But Chelsea wasn't jealous about it at all. In fact, she was all giddy about it and was as excited as we were."

"I'm not minimizing her excitement or trying to infer that she doesn't love her baby sister because of what you are seeing. What I am saying is that Chelsea has regressed to an earlier behavior pattern in order to gain attention and to feel more significant. She sees the attention her baby sister receives just from doing the things she has mastered. So by regressing to the point where she can't do things like get dressed or wipe her bottom, she is communicating in three-year-old terms her need to be taken care of. Do you follow?" I asked.

"I think I do. So what you are saying is that Chelsea acts helpless, even though we know she is not, to get my wife and me to take care of her."

"Yes, and let me pose another question to you. What feelings do you and your wife have when your daughter acts helpless?"

Taking a few moments to relive some of the recent episodes before answering, he replied, "I think we've both talked about how helpless we feel and that we should just surrender. We just give up because when we tell her she knows how to do something, she just says, 'I can't' or 'I don't know how.' We don't know how to help her. Does that make sense to you, Doc?" he asked.

"Absolute sense. Those feelings confirm for me that your daughter is looking for attention and significance and doesn't know how to go about getting it other than to impersonate the one who is getting most of it—in her eyes, that is. By taking on the defeatist attitude ('I can't do it' versus 'I won't do it'), she is pressuring you and your wife to do more for her . . ."

Finishing my sentence, he continued, ". . . and when we do more, she feels more significant and loved."

"Excellent!" I commended. "You've got it."

"Okay, thanks. Now what do I do about it?"

"The most constructive reaction for you and your wife is no reaction at all. When she says she can't get herself dressed, the best response is for you to stay placid and very matter-of-fact. Consider some psychology, such as saying that it is really too bad that she can't get dressed because you were hoping to do something special with her today. You were going to go somewhere that big girls like to go, but since she can't get dressed, maybe she's not ready to go to big girl places. Then give her a big hug, tell her you love her, and walk away. Unless I miss my guess, she will be dressed inside of two minutes.

"Zero in on the fact that she is acting in this helpless, defeatist fashion in order to gain a feeling of significance. She gets this through the attention of others, as when you do things for her that she can already do. When you toss the *big girl* bait into the water, you are fishing her out of her defeatist mind-set and into the reality that she really can do things for herself. She just has to see the motivation."

"I get it, but my wife gets her feelings hurt and feels sorry for Chelsea. Then she either ends up doing whatever it was for her or she just gives up in frustration. What should I tell her to do?"

"You should start by letting her know that she has lots of company among parents and that Chelsea's behavior is not weird or abnormal. Chelsea is doing her best to communicate that she wants more attention. If you and your wife concentrate on increasing the positive rewards when she does things the right way, and don't react when she acts helpless or like a defeatist, then you will see the misbehavior disappear relatively quickly."

Are You Experiencing a Lamb in Your Zoo?

Below is a primary list of feelings that parents experience most frequently throughout the misbehaving—discipline—resolution process with their Lamb DQ Factors. To remind you how to get started in the diagnosis process, let's go back to the technique called *projected visualization*.

Step 1

Close your eyes and clear your mind for one minute by trying not to think about anything. Try just focusing your mind's eye on a blank wall that has been painted light blue.

Step 2

Now think back to the last significant misbehaving episode with your child and relive all the various feelings you felt when you discovered the misbehavior, all the way up to the time you resolved it. Relive just those feelings for one full minute.

Step 3

Now take all of those thoughts and feelings and sum them up in one or two words that best describe your emotions at the time.

Step 4

Now search the list of emotions below to see if any of these emotions match (or come close) to the emotions you last experienced while your child was misbehaving. The highlighted section contains the words most commonly used by parents of Lambs to describe their disciplinary feelings.

PERC (PARENT'S EMOTIONAL RESPONSE CHART)
FOR USE IN DETERMINING CHILD'S DQ FACTOR

DQ FACTOR #1—BEARS

Threatened

Challenged

Angry

DQ FACTOR #2—MONKEYS

Irritated

Annoyed

Controlled

DQ FACTOR #3—PORCUPINES

Hurt

Manipulated

Minimized

DQ FACTOR #4—LAMBS

Inadequate

Pity

Frustrated

Helpless / Hopeless

If you found any of your answers under DQ Factor #4—Lambs, then you have your first affirmative indication that your child or teenager may be of this DQ Factor.

Just as you used the earlier test to determine if you are living with a Porcupine, take a few moments to collect your thoughts and take DQ Factor #4—Lamb FED-UP test *(Feelings Experienced During Unruly Periods)*. As you do so, continue (as you did above) to monitor your feelings in regard to your child's last misbehaving episode. Tune in particularly to how you felt during and after the disciplinary process. By paying attention to your feelings, the FED-UP test should help you in diagnosing your child's specific DQ Factor.

PARENT FEELING EVALUATION FOR DQ FACTOR #4 TEST

The key to this test is to try to be as objective as you can in your answers. Likewise, don't be concerned with how you perceive the test is going for your child. No one but you and your spouse should ever see the results from this test, so it does no good to try to make it look better. The value of this test is in determining a *true* score and not a *hopeful* one.

FED-UP INSTRUCTIONS

Read the following questions carefully. Each has been designed to correspond to both children and teenagers. Sometimes it is helpful to answer the questions while imagining that you are actually someone else, but someone who knows every intimate detail about you and your family. Answer the questions by circling

(a) if you *strongly agree* with the statement,

(b) if you *somewhat agree* with the statement, or

(c) if you *do not agree* with the statement.

DQ FACTOR #4—LAMB FED-UP TEST

When my child or teenager misbehaves and I confront the behavior with discipline, I feel the following:

1. Sometimes I get the feeling s/he is manipulating me to do something for her/him out of guilt.
   Circle one: (a)   (b)   (c)

2. I get very frustrated with my child because s/he comes off as being helpless.
   Circle one: (a)   (b)   (c)

3. I sometimes feel manipulated by my child when I ask her/him to do things and s/he acts helpless.
   Circle one: (a)   (b)   (c)

4. When my child misbehaves, I sometimes get the feeling s/he wants me to feel sorry for her/him.
   Circle one: (a)   (b)   (c)

5. I feel manipulated at times that my child takes advantage of my easygoing or good nature.
   Circle one: (a)   (b)   (c)

6. Sometimes I feel frustrated more than anything else when s/he misbehaves.
   Circle one: (a)   (b)   (c)

7. Sometimes I think to myself, *If you only knew how much I do for you, you would never treat me this way.*
   Circle one: (a)   (b)   (c)

8. I get the sense my child thinks of her/himself as a failure.
   Circle one: (a)   (b)   (c)

9. More often than I'd care to admit, I feel like a failure as a parent.
   Circle one: (a)   (b)   (c)

10. I feel guilty that I should do more to build my child's self-esteem.
    Circle one: (a)   (b)   (c)

---

11. Sometimes I just think I am at my wit's end when it comes to my child.
    Circle one: (a)   (b)   (c)

---

12. I hate it, but I find myself criticizing my child too much. But I just don't know what to do.
    Circle one: (a)   (b)   (c)

---

13. Sometimes I get really sad and down after scolding or disciplining my child.
    Circle one: (a)   (b)   (c)

---

14. I just sit back and assume s/he will grow out of this phase.
    Circle one: (a)   (b)   (c)

---

15. I worry that, because it seems as though I'm nagging her/him all the time, it will cause her to avoid me.
    Circle one: (a)   (b)   (c)

---

16. I try to be more encouraging, but it is so hard with this child.
    Circle one: (a)   (b)   (c)

---

17. Getting him/her to talk when we are alone can be like pulling teeth.
    Circle one: (a)   (b)   (c)

---

18. This sounds really horrible, but sometimes I wonder if s/he is depressed.
    Circle one: (a)   (b)   (c)

---

19. I hate to say it, but sometimes I feel so inadequate as a parent.
    Circle one: (a)   (b)   (c)

---

20. It tears my heart out that I get mad and have to resort to discipline.
    Circle one: (a)   (b)   (c)

---

21. I find that I feel the most guilty when s/he cries because of something I've said or done to her/him.
    Circle one: (a)   (b)   (c)

22. S/he has this way that makes me feel guilty that I'm expecting too much.
    Circle one: (a)   (b)   (c)

23. S/he doesn't say it, but I think s/he just wants me to leave her/him alone.
    Circle one: (a)   (b)   (c)

24. I think s/he tries to manipulate me into doing things that s/he really knows how to do.
    Circle one: (a)   (b)   (c)

25. I wish I knew the secret for giving her/him a shot of confidence.
    Circle one: (a)   (b)   (c)

26. I worry that s/he is too passive and will get stepped on by other kids.
    Circle one: (a)   (b)   (c)

27. I try to act more positive, but it is hard because of his/her constant negativity.
    Circle one: (a)   (b)   (c)

28. Sometimes I feel like I'm the least effective one when it comes to dealing with my child.
    Circle one: (a)   (b)   (c)

29. After disciplining him/her, I end up being the one who feels guilty even though I've done nothing to feel guilty about.
    Circle one: (a)   (b)   (c)

30. My frustration peaks when s/he acts helpless even though I know s/he can do what I ask.
    Circle one: (a)   (b)   (c)

SCORING YOUR DQ FACTOR #4—LAMB FED-UP TEST

Add up the number of (a) answers and put the number here: ____

Add up the number of (b) answers and put the number here: ____

Add up the number of (c) answers and put the number here: ____

INTERPRETING YOUR DQ FACTOR #4—LAMB FED-UP TEST

Total number of questions   30

21 or more (a) answers

If your child or teenager scored in this DQ Factor range, although it is at the upper level for Lambs, please be careful not to leap to negative conclusions. High scores do not translate into emotional or psychological problems. They are merely a correlation of the type of discipline your child will likely respond to best.

Scoring at this level indicates a child or teenager who could be referred to as introverted, avoiding attention, and very tentative in areas of self-esteem. He or she also tends to be a loner and generally has trouble fitting in among peers.

It is also often the case that this child will frustrate a parent to the point of feeling hopeless and helpless. These feelings come about when the parent sees the child giving up on himself while the parent feels powerless to change or improve things.

When it comes to discipline and limits, this child will often evade your boundaries (even after you have set them) by playing on your sympathies. This child is a champion at making you feel sorry for him or her while convincing you that he or she could not possibly do what you had asked or expected.

This child is also adept at making you feel guilty and inadequate as a parent by acting so pitiful and helpless.

Bottom line, this child is not pitiful and helpless, but has fashioned this self-image. Although a stubborn DQ Factor score to eliminate, there is no cause for alarm.

---

13 to 20 (a) answers with 10 to 20 (b) answers

A moderate DQ Factor score, as there seemed to be more children and teenagers who scored either in upper levels or very low levels of this category. Although not as pronounced as with the score you just read, you definitely have a Lamb in your home.

Scores in this range indicate a child who sees him- or herself as being more capable than the child who scores higher, but has learned to manipulate you nonetheless. These children seem to be focused on manipulating their parent(s) into putting them down by acting far more inept, incapable, and helpless than even they see themselves. If your child scored in this level, you are likely feeling stressed and tested to the limits.

You may be interested to note that children in this category (and the category above) scored in the upper 15 percent on general IQ tests.

---

8 to 12 (a) answers with approximately 10 to 18 (b) answers

Moderate to low DQ Factor score for a Lamb, and definitely not in the class of the two scores above. The study found that many moderate to low scoring DQ Factor #3—Porcupines also scored at this level or the one below this. The reason for this is that manipulation is a common cross-characteristic of both animals.

5 to 7 (a) answers with approximately 12 to 20 (b) answers

Although an unusual pattern of both (a) and (b) answers, this combination showed up too often to overlook.

This score was found to present a false positive in 26.3 percent of the cases. In other words, one parent (usually the mom) graded the child at this level, but when the other parent evaluated the same child, the score was below this level.

Any other combination with fewer than 4 (a) answers

Definitely not a Lamb! If you did not find a moderate to dominant DQ Factor among any of the others, see below.

Note: Regardless of the number of (c) answers, they serve only to rule out this DQ Factor and do not have any special significance on their own.

VISITING THE PETERSONS

THE PETERSON FAMILY

PARENTS
Mom: Lisa
Dad: Jeff

CHILDREN
Melissa (8)
Jack (7)
Darren (6)

Of all the families we studied, no family typified the discouraged, defeatist, why-bother-even-trying way of thinking like eight-year-old Melissa. She became our prototypical Lamb.

Melissa's prowess at manipulating everyone around her to see her as helpless and in need of being rescued became legendary among us. The fact that Melissa's parents, Lisa and Jeff, agreed to record several hours of their family's daily conversations made the diagnosis that much easier. Perhaps the most curious dynamic that frequently surrounds children like Melissa and their parents is the unconscious way it all goes on. As you read the transcripts from a typical conversation between Melissa and her parents, pay particular attention to the world-class manipulation. Perhaps you will see some similarities to your own parenting situation.

To provide a little background, Melissa, the oldest of the three children, had fallen into what her parents had termed an *unusual behavior pattern*. During the initial interviews, both Mom and Dad had independently described Melissa as going from fairly confident to sort of discouraged over the period of one year. They also agreed that some time back, they would have referred to her as positive. Now, they both agreed, she was negative and mopey.

We conducted some precautionary tests to ensure that Melissa was not suffering with clinical depression. Conclusive tests pointed to the fact that she was not depressed and that we were seeing a DQ Factor #4 at work. Without a doubt, Mel (as her parents called her) was at the upper end of the DQ #4—Lambs scale.

Although it seemed possible to play any portion of any conversation between Mel and her parents to instantly hear symptoms of her DQ Factor, I chose the following recording as one you might be able to relate to in some way. This recording took place as Melissa came home following soccer practice. Her mom, Lisa, was in the kitchen preparing dinner while her father had not yet come home from work.

"Hi, Mel. How was soccer practice?"

"It was horrible! I hate it. I hate my coach! He treats me the absolute worst of everyone on the team! He is such a jerk."

"What happened *this time*, Mel? And please don't call your coach a jerk."

"He just hates me. He lets his daughter Alissa and her best friend Hannah do whatever they want. They don't have to run hard, but when I can't run hard because I've been sick, I get in trouble," she moaned.

With a tone of voice that sounded something like *Oh, here it comes again,* Lisa inquired, "What do you mean, they do whatever they want, but you get in trouble for it?"

"Never mind, 'cause you never want to hear my side anyway. You and dad always [note sweeping remark *always*, which is characteristic of DQ Factor #4] take everyone else's side against me. What time is dinner 'cause I got to call D. J. about a class project?"

Apparently deciding to let the soccer issue pass, Lisa answered, "Well, your dad gets home around 6:15, and remember I told you that we have company coming for dinner tonight. Your father's boss and his wife and son are coming. Remember? That's why I couldn't pick you up from soccer practice."

"Oh yeah. I forgot. But I don't have to hang around and talk to them, do I? I have this huge project that's due tomorrow."

"Well, no, I suppose you don't have to spend a lot of time with them. But their son is your age, and it would be nice if you spent some time playing with him. I'm sure he will be bored just sitting around listening to us. By the way, what is the class project?"

"I just found out that Mr. Kempton put us into groups the day I was sick. I'm in a group with three kids that I can't even stand, plus D. J.—who is so lazy—and this project counts for one-half of our social studies grade. This totally stinks!"

Already sensing the answer to at least half of her question, Lisa asked, "So what is this project, and when is it due?"

Destined not to disappoint, Mel replied, "We're studying California missions, and my group has to have a model built tomorrow or we all get an F."

"You've got to be kidding me," Lisa said in a tone that did nothing to hide her frustration. "I can't believe you let this go to the last minute again. You can't sit there and tell me you didn't know that you were in a group and that you had to turn in your project tomorrow. You couldn't have just learned about this today!"

"Mom, I swear! Mr. Kempton never told me anything about it, and D. J. just told me today that we were all taking parts of the project and that my part was to build the mission model."

Picking up the telephone, Lisa announced, "Okay, I'm going to call Mr. Kempton right now—you know I have his home phone number—and I'm going to verify that he never told you about this project, right? Because if he says he told you about it, you are going to be grounded for the weekend."

Whether Lisa was bluffing about calling Mr. Kempton, we'll never know, but the tactic succeeded in flushing out the truth.

"Well, Mr. K did mention that we had projects due tomorrow, but I didn't know until D. J. told me that they stuck me with doing the mission model while all they had to do was put together some stupid report. I got hosed. Mom, can you or Dad just please take me to the store so I can get the stuff I need to put the model together? I can't get an F on this."

"Mel, what do you expect us to do about this tonight? You know that we have guests. How are we supposed to take you to the store and entertain your father's boss and family? I swear, young lady, you drive me completely nuts with your procrastination."

"But Mom," Mel whined, "I can't fail this project. I've got a C in social studies now, and if I don't turn in this project tomorrow, I'm dead meat."

"What is wrong with you, Mel? Why is it that we have to go through this every single time you have a project to do? Why is it that you let everything go to the last minute and then you announce at zero hour what I have to do to save you?"

"I'm sorry, Mom, but this wasn't my fault."

"Well, you can suffer the consequences for all I care. If you don't care enough about your school grades to plan ahead, then why should I? You know, this is just like last Saturday, when you got out of bed at 9:00 for a soccer game at 9:30, and the first thing out of your mouth was that I had to stop at the store and buy snacks for the team because you forgot to tell me that it was our turn. And there we are, rushing around Von's at 9:20, trying to find a cash machine so we can buy snacks. Your procrastination is driving me insane, Mel! You let everything go to the last minute and then you want me to bail you out. Why do you always do this to me? What is wrong with you?"

About thirty seconds of silence was finally broken when Mel responded in typically manipulative, yet effective Lamb fashion. "Why do you have to yell at me, Mom? You always make me feel stupid for asking you to help me. I can't help it that you and Dad make me play club soccer and I have to go to practice three nights a week after school and then I have games on Saturday. And you know I have music lessons on Thursdays. It isn't my fault that I never have time to do homework. I can't help it that I was sick on Tuesday and that was the day that Mr. Kempton gave us our assignments. I'm sorry if I'm not as smart as the other kids and need extra help. It's like nobody cares that I get behind and don't have time to do everything. Why won't you and Dad just let me quit soccer?

That's why I get behind in class. Why are you guys ruining my life by pushing me so hard to do something I'm not even good at?"

Lisa's hesitation verified that Mel's helpless victim monologue had successfully found its target by diverting the conversation away from the mission project.

"You know that your father and I place a high value on finishing things that you start, Mel. You wanted to play soccer when the season started, so we let you play soccer. It's not fair to blame me because soccer takes a lot of time. Remember what you said about all your friends being on the team? Remember that you just had to play too? How is it that all the other girls on the team seem to do just fine with their schoolwork? Why do you think that you are the only one who can't seem to get things in on time?"

"You can ask them!" Mel protested. "Bethany and Crystal never get their homework done. In fact, they are doing ten times worse than me. And Amy is getting an F in social studies, and her mom said she could quit soccer because it was ruining her grades. *Amy's mom understands.*" [Note the masterful comparison technique designed to make her mom feel guilty and inadequate.]

"Well, we are not Amy's parents, and I don't want you quitting soccer. But maybe we can talk to your coach and find out if you have to be at all of the practices. Maybe you can miss one or two when you have too much homework. But I can't believe Amy's mom would let her quit. There must be more to the story than you are telling me."

"Amy's mom understands," Mel repeated, just to make sure her previous manipulating comparison had not missed its mark. "It's like she listens to Amy and knows when she is just too stressed out."

About fifteen seconds passed without comment from Lisa. With the instinct of a true Lamb, Mel knew the time was right to increase the manipulation.

"Please, Mom. If I don't get to Michael's [craft store] tonight, I'm dead. I know you are busy, and I'm sorry I forgot about this. I understand if you can't take me. Just let me ride my bike there after dinner. I got to get my stuff for the project."

"There is no way I am letting you ride your bike all the way to Michael's after dark, Mel. Are you nuts?" Lisa replied.

In what must have been inspired genius and was a masterpiece of parental manipulation, Mel added, "Then let me call Grandma. She's feeling better, and maybe she's going to go out tonight or whatever. She always tells me that she will help me with school projects when I'm stuck."

"No way!" Lisa protested. "You're not going to bother your grandmother about going out at night after she's been sick. I'll take you this time, and maybe your dad can help you put your model together after Mr. and Mrs. Otis leave. Get your things together, 'cause we've got to fly there and back. I'll call your father and tell him that if he gets here and we're gone, that we'll be right back. You better appreciate what I'm going through for you, Mel. I'm serious."

"Thanks, Mom," Mel replied with syrupy sweetness. "You're the best."

I smiled as I listened to the final nail being hammered into her mom's manipulation coffin. Mel had about as much trouble gaining control over her mother as Tiger Woods has playing miniature golf. In fact, if trophies were given out for championship manipulation, Mel would have a closet full of them.

ARE YOU LIVING WITH A LAMB?

Now it is time to see if you are living with a Lamb. The essential questions below were extracted from the complete DQ Factor battery of tests. Over a period of time, we found that these questions were more than sufficient to fully flush out your child's DQ Factor.

As you did with the previous test, try your best to separate yourself from any emotional investment in the answers or outcome. You can best do this by imagining you are an outsider—but one who knows your child inside and out—and you have been asked to evaluate him or her.

Read the following questions carefully. Each has been designed to correspond to any age child or teenager. Answer the questions below by circling

(a) if you *strongly agree* with the statement,

(b) if you *somewhat agree* with the statement, or

(c) if you *do not agree* with the statement.

DQ FACTOR #4—LAMB TEST

1. S/he can be very manipulative, especially in the area of trying to make me feel sorry for her/him.
   Circle one: (a) (b) (c)

2. S/he frequently stalls or puts off doing things I've told her/him to do, even though s/he knows it will cause a problem.
   Circle one: (a) (b) (c)

3. When s/he was younger, s/he would cry easily.
   Circle one: (a) (b) (c)

4. S/he would prefer to sit in an inconspicuous place in the classroom than in the front.
   Circle one: (a) (b) (c)

5. Even though I recognize that I am being manipulated, I find myself doing too many things for him/her anyway.
   Circle one: (a) (b) (c)

6. Sometimes I just get the sense that s/he wants me to think s/he is helpless.
   Circle one: (a) (b) (c)

7. S/he would definitely put off till tomorrow what should be done today.
   Circle one: (a) (b) (c)

8. It is not at all unusual for him/her to throw down a book or towel when frustrated.
   Circle one: (a)   (b)   (c)

9. When my child misbehaves, it is usually because s/he didn't do something s/he should have done rather than because s/he did something s/he shouldn't have done.
   Circle one: (a)   (b)   (c)

10. Her/his favorite excuse is, "I forgot."
    Circle one: (a)   (b)   (c)

11. When s/he gets into trouble, I rarely (if ever) see her/him owning the problem.
    Circle one: (a)   (b)   (c)

12. When it comes to taking the blame for misbehaving, s/he usually diverts it to someone else.
    Circle one: (a)   (b)   (c)

13. S/he seems to have a "poor me" way of seeing circumstances.
    Circle one: (a)   (b)   (c)

14. When things don't go her/his way, s/he shuts down rather than works on it.
    Circle one: (a)   (b)   (c)

15. S/he seemed to learn to walk on schedule.
    Circle one: (a)   (b)   (c)

16. S/he is more on the lazy side than the active side.
    Circle one: (a)   (b)   (c)

17. In schoolwork or with chores, s/he does not take much pride in the job s/he is doing.
    Circle one: (a)   (b)   (c)

18. She is more characteristic of a follower than a leader.
    Circle one: (a)   (b)   (c)

19. My child is more prone to speaking prior to thinking.
    Circle one: (a)   (b)   (c)

20. S/he was not one to sleep through the night early on.
    Circle one: (a)   (b)   (c)

21. As an infant, s/he cried more often than my other children did, or more than I'd heard was normal.
    Circle one: (a)   (b)   (c)

22. S/he makes me feel like I demand too much of her/him.
    Circle one: (a)   (b)   (c)

23. S/he seems more comfortable sitting at home than going out to play.
    Circle one: (a)   (b)   (c)

24. S/he is a smart child and could get much better grades.
    Circle one: (a)   (b)   (c)

25. I feel manipulated at times that my child takes advantage of my easygoing or good nature.
    Circle one: (a)   (b)   (c)

26. I feel frustrated more than anything else when s/he misbehaves.
    Circle one: (a)   (b)   (c)

27. Giving her/him time-outs doesn't seem to phase him/her.
    Circle one: (a)   (b)   (c)

28. S/he enjoys attention from me and a few others, but not being the center of attention.
    Circle one: (a)   (b)   (c)

29. S/he has no idea how much extra I go out of my way to accommodate her/him.
    Circle one: (a)   (b)   (c)

30. S/he seems ungrateful or unappreciative of all the things I do for her/him.
Circle one: (a) (b) (c)

31. S/he probably sees her/himself as more of a failure than a success.
Circle one: (a) (b) (c)

32. I feel like a marginal parent more often than I'd care to admit.
Circle one: (a) (b) (c)

33. S/he has lower self-esteem than I would like to see in her/him.
Circle one: (a) (b) (c)

34. Sometimes I just think I am at my wit's end when it comes to my child.
Circle one: (a) (b) (c)

35. S/he seemed to learn to talk on schedule.
Circle one: (a) (b) (c)

36. S/he drives me to the point where I know I'm being too critical.
Circle one: (a) (b) (c)

37. S/he seems to lack the self-confidence of other children her/his own age.
Circle one: (a) (b) (c)

38. Any discipline I give seems to make me feel worse than her/him.
Circle one: (a) (b) (c)

39. I think this is just a phase s/he will grow out of.
Circle one: (a) (b) (c)

40. S/he seems to avoid situations that can be demanding or even the least bit confrontational.
Circle one: (a) (b) (c)

41. I try to be more encouraging, but it is so hard with this child.
Circle one: (a)   (b)   (c)

42. S/he seems to get her/his way more often than the others.
Circle one: (a)   (b)   (c)

43. Getting him/her to talk when we are alone can be like pulling teeth.
Circle one: (a)   (b)   (c)

44. S/he comes across as depressed and down more than excited and up.
Circle one: (a)   (b)   (c)

45. S/he has a way of making me feel like I'm letting her/him down.
Circle one: (a)   (b)   (c)

46. After being disciplined, s/he tends to isolate or stay away from me.
Circle one: (a)   (b)   (c)

47. I wish s/he would stand up for her/his rights more.
Circle one: (a)   (b)   (c)

48. I think that s/he cries more to manipulate me than because s/he is really hurting.
Circle one: (a)   (b)   (c)

49. There is no doubt in my mind that s/he is much more capable than s/he would like others to believe.
Circle one: (a)   (b)   (c)

50. S/he doesn't say it as much as s/he acts like s/he just wants to be left alone.
Circle one: (a)   (b)   (c)

51. I think s/he was more difficult to toilet train than most.
Circle one: (a)   (b)   (c)

52. S/he plays this role or game that s/he can't do things for her/himself.
    Circle one: (a)   (b)   (c)

53. S/he seems to lack self-confidence.
    Circle one: (a)   (b)   (c)

54. I've seen situations where other kids have taken advantage of her/him because of her/his good nature.
    Circle one: (a)   (b)   (c)

55. S/he doesn't seem to get bored too easily and can spend considerable time doing one thing.
    Circle one: (a)   (b)   (c)

56. S/he has a glass-is-half-empty versus half-full way of seeing things.
    Circle one: (a)   (b)   (c)

57. When her/his feelings are hurt, s/he is more likely to retreat than to confront.
    Circle one: (a)   (b)   (c)

58. S/he does not do well with people in authority (teachers, coaches, etc.).
    Circle one: (a)   (b)   (c)

59. If I had to choose between describing her/his personality type as being either avoidant or confrontational, I'd say definitely avoidant.
    Circle one: (a)   (b)   (c)

60. I wonder if his/her *helpless* or *I just can't do it* routine is just an act.
    Circle one: (a)   (b)   (c)

SCORING YOUR DQ FACTOR #4—LAMB TEST

Add up the number of (a) answers and put the number here: _____

Add up the number of (b) answers and put the number here: _____

Add up the number of (c) answers and put the number here: _____

INTERPRETING YOUR CHILD'S/TEENAGER'S DQ #4 TEST

Total number of questions   60

47 or more (a) answers with approximately 13 (b) answers

As a precursor, it is important to keep these scores in perspective. If your child or teenager scored high in this DQ Factor, be careful not to leap to conclusions. High scores do not translate into emotional or psychological problems, nor are they an indicator of intelligence. They are merely a correlation of the type of discipline your child will likely respond to best.

Scores at the upper end of this scale produced a fascinating split in the motives of Lambs. Those who scored at the high end were considerably more manipulative than those even at the next level down. Even more fascinating was that they were more motivated to get others to see them as helpless so that they would not have demands made of them. In other words, their driving force was to be left alone.

The second group of Lambs (in this category as well as the next, below) also saw themselves as weak and somewhat incapable, but they were more motivated to manipulate their parents into doing things for them than to be left alone.

Kids with scores at this level also scored high on insecurity scales. It is this child's insecurity that drives his need to be comforted (or even controlled), which helps him to gain a sense of well-being, significance, and of course, love.

Because Lambs are not as outgoing as Monkeys, as confrontational as Bears, or as aggressive as Porcupines, they find it easiest to gain your attention by appearing weak, needy, and unable to do things that you would expect them to be able to do.

We also found that kids and teens at this range frequently and purposely sabotaged things like tasks, assignments, or chores to reinforce your perception that you are asking too much of them.

---

33 to 46 (a) answers with approximately 13 to 17 (b) answers

Moderately high Lamb DQ Factor. This child is definitely seeking your attention by manipulation. Unlike the subjects who scored higher, these children are not trying to be left alone as much as they are trying to be seen as dependent and incapable and therefore in need of your help.

Interestingly enough, we found that children and teens at this level truly saw themselves as weaker and unable to do for themselves, whereas the group who scored higher were clearly more manipulative and knew they could do more, but chose not to.

An odd pattern emerged when these children and teens were given standard IQ tests. We found that approximately 62 percent of the group scored at or slightly above average, while the other 48 percent tested in the upper one-tenth of IQ range. Try as we might, we were unable to come up with a satisfactory theory for this IQ pattern.

Bottom line, very smart and manipulative kids are a handful.

---

18 to 32 (a) answers with approximately 10 to 14 (b) answers

Moderate DQ Factor for the average Lamb. Scores in this range tend to be significantly less manipulative and genuinely see themselves through critical eyes.

These kids tend to come from parents who are perfectionistic and somewhat more critical and/or demanding than most parents. As a result, they tend to lie more than any of the other DQ Factors. This is likely because they are already struggling with a negative self-image and are trying to conceal perceived faults by not telling the truth if they think it might lead to criticism.

Although these kids tested right down the middle in IQ tests, they tested in the upper third in an area called *intrapersonal relationships*. This area measures personal insights and the ability to self-analyze and to be introspective. These are the gifts of people who often end up in helping professions such as therapists, pastors, teachers, and doctors.

---

8 to 17 (a) answers with approximately 5 to 12 (b) answers

Low DQ Factor range. Kids in this range were common. In fact, it is not at all unusual for a child who scored in the low to moderate range as a Porcupine to also score in the low to moderate range as a Lamb.

Children in this range tended to be slightly introverted with a little lower than normal self-esteem.

---

7 or fewer (a) answers

Definitely not a Lamb.

Note: Regardless of the number of (c) answers, they serve only to rule out this DQ Factor and do not have any special significance on their own.

THE DQ RX FOR LAMBS

As you've seen with the three previous DQ Factors, there is a lengthy continuum of disciplinary techniques that parents have at their disposal whenever their child has broken a rule or stepped over a boundary. One of the primary objectives of the study was to focus on and identify both the ineffective and effective disciplinary techniques used with specific DQ Factors. My team and I found it remarkable that the majority of parents repeatedly utilized nearly identical methods of discipline—even when that discipline proved to be ineffective.

The list below comprises the disciplinary methods most frequently used by parents of Lambs. The list is separated by type of discipline and effectiveness. In this situation, effectiveness refers to both an objective and subjective percentage we assigned to each discipline type as we witnessed its implementation and overall success rate in creating behavioral changes among DQ Factor #4—Lambs.

Type of Discipline with DQ Factor #4—Lambs	Effectiveness
AGGRESSIVE SPANKING	17 PERCENT

This term referred to any spanking technique that ranged from taking the child's pants down to spank him with an open palm, to utilizing a spanking instrument such as a wooden spoon, wooden hanger, paddle, etc. Again, for the record, I am not against a light swat on the child's bottom with an open palm. However, the line of excessive correction can be much more easily crossed when any instrument is used in conjunction with spanking.

We found aggressive spanking to be one of the least effective discipline methods used with Lambs. The reason for this seemed to lie in the fact that Lambs routinely struggled with self-esteem issues, which caused them to withdraw just by sheer nature. When a harsh correction was added to the mix, their insecurities and feelings of persecution were exacerbated.

Note: There were no abuse issues throughout the study. Societal standards still view spanking with objects that do not leave permanent marks to be acceptable. For the record, I am not opposed to spanking, but I am opposed to using any instrument (spoons, hangers, belts, etc.) to spank children. Utilizing these items depersonalizes the discipline process and can clearly inflict excessive and unintentional injury.

SIMPLE SWATTING   25 PERCENT

This term refers to a spanking technique that would be called a simple swat (or series of swats) to the child's behind, delivered by an open hand to the outside of the pants and/or underwear. Simple swats on a Lamb's behind were only marginally more effective than their more aggressive counterpart above. The same rationale as above should be noted.

IGNORING   69 PERCENT

Ignoring is the premeditated practice of not letting your child's attention-seeking misbehaviors get to you.

For instance, when your Lamb acts out in a clear effort to get you to rescue him, the rule of ignoring simply states to continue doing what you are doing. In short, you adopt a position that *it is no big deal.*

Don't let your child see that he has gotten to you, or he will continue to pull the strings and you will continue to come to his rescue. Ignoring also requires you to be in control of your nonverbal signals (facial expressions, sighs, groans, etc.).

The reason that ignoring is generally effective with Lamb DQ Factors is that it transfers the power from your child, who is "hooking" you into coming to his rescue, back to you by ignoring the behavior. The caveat to ignoring is that you must not do it out of anger or in a punitive or withholding way. It is one thing to let the misbehavior pass without making a big deal of it. It is another, and much more damaging, thing to make your child feel as though you do not care about him.

VERBAL REPRIMANDS   23 PERCENT

Lambs were difficult to evaluate when verbal reprimands were applied as a disciplinary technique. At first it appeared that they stopped the troublesome behavior and became more compliant. Shortly after, however, the Lamb seemed to feed off the verbal reprimand in that it served to reinforce his already negative self-image. Ultimately we concluded that nonharsh reprimands were fine as short-term, temporary ways of getting the child to stop a certain behavior, but as the verbal reprimand took on a more personal or demeaning tone, the less effective it became.

ROOM TIME-OUTS 19 PERCENT

Lambs are not nearly the social creatures that Monkeys, Bears, and even Porcupines are. Therefore, removing your Lamb from proximity of the family (and therefore relationships) through the application of time-outs proved to be a mixed bag of results.

When the Lamb was sent to his room for any extended period of time (generally over 15 minutes), we found that the punishment had minimal, and in some cases, detrimental effects.

Lambs are already motivated to shrink away and withdraw from relationships because of their poor self-image and avoidance of criticism. When they act out, it is often their subconscious desire to be rescued and pulled into relationship, and thereby receive affirmation that you still love them and they are significant. When you remove the Lamb from interaction with you (and others) by putting him in his room, his negative self-image is reinforced. In short, he believes he is unlovable, and therefore the likelihood of his continuing to act out to prove it increases.

PROXIMITY TIME-OUTS 72 PERCENT

See Rx #1 (page 236)

RESTRICTIONS 22 PERCENT

Restricting Lambs to their rooms or homes produced mixed (and suspect) results. A few Lambs responded well to being placed on restriction—if they were generally confined to home for a weekend. Whenever the restriction involved being placed in their room for any extended period of time, several Lambs actually began to seek revenge against the punishing and emotionally withholding parent. We found that Lambs who assumed this more hostile Porcupine trait were among the most difficult DQ Factors to work with.

TAKING AWAY PRIVILEGES   77 PERCENT

Taking away privileges such as TV, stereo, or bike proved to be an effective tool with Lambs.

Because this DQ Factor relies so heavily on outside stimuli to distract him from dealing with his insecurities, removing important things such as TV, stereo, video games, sports, or clubs following a behavior problem served as a healthy deterrent against future violations. The second reason that taking away privileges was as effective as it was stemmed from its connection to natural consequences. For example, if your child forgot to do his chores because he was engrossed with playing games on his Gameboy, taking away the game serves as the natural consequence.

A smart technique to employ when you can is to place the forbidden item in view to serve as a reminder. In the above example, placing the Gameboy next to the trash poses a strong psychological image that will hopefully stick with him longer than tossing it into a drawer. Keep in mind that the key is to do all of this in a calm, matter-of-fact manner.

BELITTLING   0 PERCENT

Completely ineffective! If you set out to destroy your child's emotional security and sense of well-being (especially among DQ Factor #4—Lambs), belittling would definitely be your first choice.

THREATS   23 PERCENT

Making a threat is what you do when you have run out of ideas, and one of the pervasive feelings experienced by parents of Lambs is *I give up*.

Because Lambs can be so exasperating, we found that many parents resorted to making threats in an effort to get their kids to comply and behave.

Go back to the basic tenet of discipline:
#1—A limit is only a request unless it carries consequences.
#2—The consequences must be communicated and fully understood by your child.
#3—You must follow through with the consequence after you have given your word.

NATURAL CONSEQUENCES   77 PERCENT

Natural consequences seemed like the universal antidote to most disciplinary situations faced by parents regardless of their child's DQ Factor.

Natural consequences are effective
because they are rooted and grounded
in biblical truths of reaping and sowing.
With children, the sooner we teach them
that choosing to do X will always produce Y,
the sooner they are likely to stop doing X.

Please refer to the Rx section below to
discover more about the power of
implementing natural consequences.

The DQ Rx

In addition to the insights gained by examining the aforementioned typical types of discipline used in conjunction with DQ Factor Lambs, our research also produced some other effective boundary and discipline techniques. We found the following Rx actions and ideas to be powerful in neutralizing the pesky little misbehaving characteristics of Lambs.

Rx #1

Proximity Time-outs

This time-out hybrid was created especially for DQ Factor #4—Lambs due to their schizoid tendencies. In case *schizoid* is a new term to you, it broadly describes a person whose personality type tends to avoid people, dislikes confrontation, and is as much a loner as a Monkey is a party animal. Schizoid types often feel alone, insecure, and insignificant, and prefer to be left alone. As you can see, restricting—or even just giving this child a time-out where he is secluded—feeds into his schizoid tendencies. The correct path is to gently pull these kids into social activities and not to further isolate them.

A proximity time-out (PT) simply means accomplishing the isolating benefits of the time-out while avoiding the separation aspects. Flash back to the weird pre-1970s when teachers actually had control of their students through the support of parents and administrators, and when "Go sit in the corner until I tell you to come out" was employed. The subtle genius of this time-out was that it didn't ostracize the child from his classmates by sending him out of the room. It succeeded in creating an emotional distance without creating a physical distance. That way, the defeatist-minded child wasn't faced with being alone with his own self-destructive thoughts.

So as PTs apply to you, feel free to try placing a chair in the corner of the kitchen or family room where your child can sit facing the wall. Don't leave the room, as that creates a different dynamic. The goal is for you to be in the room—cooking, watching TV, or reading—while your Lamb studies the wallpaper. Again, don't do this for extended periods of time. Fifteen minutes is sufficient for grade-school children, while fifteen months is sufficient for teenagers. (Just wanted to see if you were paying attention.) In actuality, the PT technique is *not* recommended for teens.

Rx #2
NATURAL CONSEQUENCES

Let's start with the mutual understanding that natural consequences are going to be really tough for you if you happen to be the parent of a Lamb. I say this because Lamb parents tend to have two to three dozen more caretaker genes than other parents. Let me save you a trip to the library—there are no such things as caretaker genes. But if they did exist, they would be those internal drivers that keep you from letting your child fail, fall, or experience hurt and consequences.

Parents of Lambs have the toughest time letting their children fail. One theory is that they are perfectionists and don't want it to reflect poorly on them. On the other hand, I believe it is that these parents are simply so enmeshed with their children that they can't stand the thought of their co-experiencing any pain. In theory, *his pain* becomes *my pain.*

Let me give you a prime example of how natural consequences should work with Lambs. I worked with the family of a seventh-grade boy who was struggling in school. His grades had slipped to the level where his baseball coach said that he wouldn't be able to play unless he brought them up.

After thoroughly testing him, we determined that he did not have any learning disorder. If he had any disorder at all, it was laziness, and the last time I checked, laziness was not a diagnosis. The father and mother were so enmeshed with him that they would not let him experience the natural consequence of poor grades: no baseball. Whenever he forgot to bring a book home from school to study, they would drive to school and get it. If he had too much homework, they would cancel their plans and stay home to help. Whatever it took, he wasn't going to fail and thus not be able to play on the team. Why? Because the baseball team had taken on too much importance to both the child and his parents.

My recommendation was to stop rewarding the boy's laziness and forget-fulness by insulating him from failure. If he lacked the personal motivation to keep his grades up, why should the parents care more than he did? For several weeks they related that they had full intentions of letting him suffer the natural consequences of his actions, only to come to his rescue at the last moment.

I showed them how they were setting up their child for a life of failure. By not allowing him to experience the embarrassments, disappointments, and losses created by his choices, they were teaching him that he is not responsible for his decisions. They just could not seem to grasp the gravity of their codependent decisions and how what appears to be a relatively small thing today (homework) can turn into a lifetime of helplessness while expecting others to rescue him.

If you are considering the application of natural consequences for the first time, you will want to put your child on notice. Putting him on notice means telling him what is coming. Otherwise, you are setting everyone up for failure. As you may recall in a previous chapter, I strongly favor presenting your boundary and limit commitments in writing to your child well in advance of perceived challenges. This puts your child on notice that you intend to let him fail and accept the natural consequence for his action. Doing this in a matter-of-fact, nonthreatening, or sarcastic manner gives your child a sense that failing to comply means he is choosing the punishment.

As a word of caution, NCs are not an option in every misbehaving circumstance. If your young child particularly enjoys touching the stove while you are cooking, it isn't a viable option to stand back and wait for him to burn himself. In situations like these, you would shift to a logical consequence.

Rx #3
LOGICAL CONSEQUENCES

Logical consequences are the disciplinary techniques that you employ when the natural consequences could lead to danger. For instance, in the hot stove situation above, you might take three bowls filled with three varying temperatures of water: mild, warm, and hot—with the hottest being uncomfortable, but not hot enough to hurt him. Let your child place his fingers in the three bowls. When he gets to the hottest bowl, you would lovingly reinforce how much hotter the stove is and how much it would hurt if he touched it in the wrong place.

Both natural and logical consequences worked very effectively with Lambs.

Rx #4
THE THREE TIMES, ONE LAMB STUDY

The world of advertising has taught psychology a valuable lesson about the mind and how it receives gross impressions. To put your mind at ease, a *gross impression* is not what happens when your child walks in on you in the bathroom, but a term that relates to how many times the mind has to experience something before it stores it in long-term memory. Advertisers have learned that the brain has to see a commercial approximately seven times before it recognizes the product, message, and the call to action (the reason to buy it).

As gross impressions apply to parenting your Lamb, we tested a theory whereby we asked parents to go a full week of forcing themselves to compliment their child for each negative or corrective comment they made. We had some families on a one-to-one *compliment-to-correction ratio*, while others were on more aggressive ratios up to as high as seven-to-one. To give you an example, if Mom said, "Why do you do this to me? I told you to pick up your clothes an hour ago," then she was responsible for catching her child in the act of doing something right (within an hour) and to follow that with saying a positive. Yes, it can be a challenge to catch your child doing something right that frequently, but you can do it.

We found that the Lambs who received the one-to-one and two-to-one compliment-to-correction ratios showed a 27 percent improvement in compliance. However, the Lambs who received a three-to-one compliment-to-correction ratio produced a 52 percent improvement quotient. To put it in nonmathematical terms, if you catch your child doing something *right*, and you compliment him on it three times more often than you criticize him or correct him, he is going to be WAY EASIER TO DEAL WITH.

And just to finish the thought, we found that the higher ratios (up to seven-to-one) did not produce significantly higher returns. Therefore, we came away recommending a solid three-to-one return on your complimenting investment to be exactly what the doctor ordered.

Rx #5

Disregarding

Disregarding is a powerful psychological tool that most parents don't even know about. While it was an amazingly successful tool with Bears and Monkeys, it had slightly less impact with Lambs, but is still highly recommended.

The theory behind disregarding is that if misbehavior is not reinforced (at least occasionally), it will lose its importance and then die under its own weight. Keep in mind that even negative reinforcement (criticism, yelling, punishment) is reinforcement.

The trick to disregarding is that you must practice it each time the behavior occurs if you want it to go away. Let me give you an example of how disregarding works among Lambs. A concern of Lamb parents is how frequently they hear their child express harsh and critical things about him or herself. If you listened to as many tapes and read as many transcripts as we did, you could see it unfold too. Each time the Lamb said something like, "I'm stupid," or "I can't do that," you could predict the parents' rescuing response. Parents of Lambs find themselves so caught up in overcoming their child's perceived negativity and need-to-be-made-to-feel-better cycle, that they mindlessly respond.

Remember the temperamental candy machine example in chapter 7? If the machine refused to give the merchandise or return your money, you would eventually give up. However, if after your abusive tirade against the machine, it coughed up either your money or your candy bar, you could bet your life that you would kick and poke that machine every time you had a problem with it—maybe even for fun on Fridays. Why? Because you would have assumed that your candy-dislodging actions had worked.

RX #6

Unconditional Love

I hesitate to use this term at all because I think that all love, short of the love we experience from God, has at least some conditions placed on it. As much as we would like to say that our love for our children is unconditional, one would have to admit that there is some extreme point where love is no longer unconditional. Not to belabor the issue, but imagine you have a teenager or adult child who is just a horrible, hurtful person and goes out of his way to cause you and others intense pain. At some point, the unconditional love you felt for him as a child has now turned conditional.

Now that we have examined the esoteric sense of the term *unconditional love*, let's take a look at it regarding your child. The DQ Factor study provided many surprises, but none shocked us to the degree of finding out how many parents do not tell their children how much and why they love them. In fully 24 percent of the families taking part in the study, we never heard either parent tell their children he or she loved them. This is unconscionable with all children, but is the most damaging to DQ Factor #4—Lambs because of their intense insecurities.

With that in mind, I want to give you a formula that I have found to work miracles with my family, as well as with hundreds of others. My simple formula is accessible to every parent and involves just four cornerstone concepts:

Concept #1   Call home once a day (dads especially) after school or whenever, and make it a point to talk with each child.

Concept #2   Now comes the hard part for some parents. Do not (repeat, *do not*) hang up before telling your children that you love them. I realize it can be tough at first, as it didn't come naturally to me either. In a very short time, however, it became second nature. The result is that my kids learned to say, "I love you," back to my wife and me with complete ease, even if they are in front of their teenage friends.

Concept #3 Now comes the second hardest thing for some parents. You must (repeat, *must*) hug your children. My children have grown up knowing that hugs, "I love you," and compliments (see below) go together. In my family, hugging moments include, but are not limited to: before I go out the door to work or they to school, when we first connect back up in the evening, whenever they do something significant, and when they go to bed. Hugs communicate security, love, and acceptance and are a million (not clinically supported) times more powerful than a kiss.

Concept #4 If you and I were to spend ten or fifteen minutes just casually talking, I assure you I would find at least five things about you that are truly remarkable. Let's say that I learned you volunteer your time once a month to participate in your church's program to feed the homeless. Now consider how you would feel if, as we were saying goodbye, I said, "You know, I am really impressed with how much you give of yourself to your church in spite of the fact that you are so busy with your family. You are truly remarkable!" My sense is that you would feel two things: First, you would feel proud of yourself; and second, you would feel good about me for noticing and complimenting you.

Now let's turn this into a parenting paradigm. Let's say you called home at 4:00 and learned that your daughter made an 89 on a tough test. At the end of your conversation you say, "You know, I am really impressed that you got that good of a grade on your test today. You have been so busy, but you still found the time to study. You are truly remarkable!" Can you imagine how your child feels about you and what this does for her self-image?

The purpose of these four concepts is to cement a loving, caring, and kindness bond between you and your child. When that bond is in place, discipline becomes much, much, much (not enough time or pages to expand on how *much*) easier.

In conclusion, when you talk with your kids (and spouse), focus your vocabulary on the extreme complimentary words like: *remarkable, impressive, wonderful, talented, special*, and *amazing*.

Rx #7

THE MIRACLE OF TRADITION

Even though we have touched on the quality-time issue in a couple of areas in this book, I think this term has been so overused in parenting circles that it has lost its significance. Let me tell you about tradition and why I call it a miracle.

Please don't get the notion that I am any sort of genius, because I stumbled onto this concept quite by accident. When my kids were small (first grade), my wife and I found that it was difficult to get them energized in the mornings. After they grabbed a quick breakfast and had their lunchboxes packed, we usually had about ten minutes before it was carpool time. Those minutes became the most powerful minutes of the day because we played. Most of the time we went outside and kicked the soccer ball between the three of us (my wife watched), or we played catch or shot baskets or just wrestled. This accomplished several powerful things, but in particular, it got their day started with fun and laughter and put the right spin on their morning. It also served to bond them to me and to make me feel great about what I was providing them emotionally.

Now fast-forward to the first day my daughter started high school. Because she was now a mature woman (ha), kicking the soccer ball in the yard before school wasn't going to happen anymore. So on her first day, we left an extra twenty minutes early and stopped at a bagel and coffee shop near her high school. My job was simple: Buy her hot chocolate and a bagel and make conversation with her for twenty minutes. Oh, and all the better if I could make her laugh a few times before dropping her off to school.

One of my favorite ways of making her laugh was to drop her off in front of her friends. As I was pulling away from the curb, I'd roll the window down and announce, "Oh, I forgot . . . I love you!" I laugh now even as I am writing this because five years later, I still picture her huge, embarrassed smile and cute giggle. Don't think for a second that she didn't love it. And occasionally, just as she reached her group of friends, it was tremendous fun to call out that she forgot to take her Flintstone vitamin.

Back to the point, we made a tradition of going to that same bagel place for four years solid. We were talking about it, and I think that the flu and travel schedules caused us to miss a grand total of five days in four years. I can't take credit for this quality time we spent being the reason that she was an honors student and senior class president, but I can tell you that it improved the quality of life for both of us. And just so you don't think I favored my daughter and abandoned my son, he joined us every day when he started at the same high school, and we are continuing to this moment. He isn't nearly as fun to tease with the Flintstone vitamin bit, because he just turns around and announces, "No, I took my Dino vitamin this morning—but I love you anyway, Dad."

In case you are wondering about specific DQ Factors and traditions—this concept is a miracle worker with all DQ Factors, but especially with Lambs. Please, do not make the mistake some parents make by thinking you can sit at the table for twenty minutes and read your paper or make cell-phone calls. This is a sin. Recognize this time as a gift from God, and use it wisely.

Rx #8

BEING POSITIVE

Perhaps by now you have noticed that I am basically a positive person. It is, however, important to disclose that I have to work hard at it. My nature is to be a bit on the moody and introspective (Lamb) side. I reveal this so that those of you who have personalities like mine will understand that you have complete control over your moods and how you are perceived. Being positive is a choice, and the day I realized that was the day I figured out that I do not have the right to inflict my *mood du jour* on my wife and kids. You can decide to be positive, or you can decide to be negative. Either will have a significant impact on your kids.

Lambs thrive and grow best in a positive environment where compliments, love, and encouragement abound. Choosing this environment may be tougher for you in the short term, but you will soon prefer it, and so will your family.

Rx #9

PUTTING YOUR LAMB TO WORK (THE DECK OF CHORES)

Back for a repeat performance with Lambs!

You may recall from our discussion how effective The Deck of Chores was with the other DQ Factors. It proved even more effective with Lambs because it takes the parent out of the "bad guy" role.

This is the ingenious idea that employs between ten and fifty blank four-by-six cards. On each card write a different chore on one side and the card number on the reverse. Make sure you write age-appropriate chores for your child so you do not have your five-year-old up on the roof with your pneumatic hammer, replacing the shingles.

When your child misbehaves and it is time to decide on his discipline, we found that a visit to The Deck of Chores was both entertaining and effective, but it did something for each DQ Factor that we had not anticipated. Because the child was the one to select a discipline chore from the deck, he could not really blame the parent for making him do something he hated to do. Remember, Lambs seek pity and to be rescued. When he chooses his chore consequence, he has no one to blame.

Rx #10
REFLECTIVE LISTENING

The fine art of reflective listening requires you to listen and then reflect back to your child what you heard from him or her. This is a marvelous technique in that it:

(a) slows the conversation down to a manageable pace,

(b) requires you to listen, and

(c) allows your child to better hear what he is saying, as it is coming from someone other than himself.

A reflective listening technique would sound something like this:

"So Matt, you are saying you think it is unfair that you can't ride your bicycle to the mall."

Now come the four most powerful words in the English language:

"So help me to understand why you think it is safe to ride your bike in that kind of traffic and at night."

As you can see, reflective listening allows your child to engage you in a dialogue rather than defending what he wants to do, while being sure that you are not just being mean and arbitrary. Anytime you engage your children in conversation, you are empowering them to think past the obvious ("because I want to") and to at least hear your side. Doing so is the only effective method to healthy communication.

A FINAL VIEW OF THE LAMB ZOO

As lovable as they are cute, Lambs can be the most heartwrenching of the DQ Factors. They don't wear you down and drive you to blood pressure medicine like Bears, Monkeys, and Porcupines, but they do cause you to question your parenting skills.

Lambs are really special children. They are as bright, insightful, and sweet as they are challenging. Hopefully, the advice and the success quotients attached to disciplinary techniques will help you handle your little Lamb.

CHAPTER 10

AN EMPTY CORNER IN THE DQ ZOO?

CHILDREN WITHOUT DOMINANT DQ FACTORS

A most curious fact cropped up while classifying and categorizing our four dominant DQ Factor animals. Although only 7.3 percent of the kids twelve and under (no teenagers) participating in the survey met the criteria, a fifth DQ Factor emerged nevertheless. Even after independent evaluators and family members evaluated these kids for the DQ Factors, they still tested out to be what we termed "nonspecific." This term simply meant that, try as we might, 7.3 percent of those tested displayed tendencies (or symptoms) of two or more DQ Factors. Some even demonstrated all four DQ Factors. These kids were a most interesting anomaly. In fact, they were so interesting, we began referring to them as DQ Factor #5—Zebras.

We attached the Zebra label to these children because of the changes a Zebra foal goes through on its way to adolescence. For instance, did you know that Zebra foals are born with brown stripes that elongate and gradually turn to black as the animal approaches its teen years? Whereas our DQ Factor #5 kids failed to produce stripes, they did begin to show emerging DQ patterns even during the relatively short time we were with them. To clarify, though none of the 7.3 percent could be positively identified with any single DQ Factor when the study began, several had begun to evolve as it was concluding. In short, their stripes were changing.

Although the study was not set up to follow these kids through their childhood and into adolescence, we did note a few remarkable similarities among our Zebras. They were as follows:

- Of the 7.3 percent nonspecific DQ Factor subjects, 60 percent were girls.
- The most common age group among the DQ Factor #5—Zebras were

   Girls between the ages of 4 and 7;

   Boys between the ages of 3 and 6.
- Zebras began to emerge with one of the dominant DQ Factors (Bears, Monkeys, Porcupines, or Lambs) the closer they got to eight years old.
- The most common combination of DQ Factors started with Lambs with mixtures of other DQ traits.
- Zebras, although they had no dominant DQ Factor type, were just as normal as the other children participating in the study. There was no connection whatsoever between this phenomena and any emotional or psychological issues.

Even though our study was not designed to stay with these kids long enough to see a dominant DQ Factor emerge, I still was able to put forth a theory—that most of these kids will emerge as Porcupines with perhaps some Bear tendencies. I make this prediction based on the fact that these kids responded best to the disciplinary tips given to parents of Porcupines.

In summary, if you have a child without a clear-cut specific and dominant DQ Factor, you should first practice the advice given to parents of the DQ Factor Porcupines. The odds are, your Zebra will respond just fine.

EPILOGUE

ERASERS, WHITE-OUT, AND PAINT REMOVER

I go back to the point I made at the beginning of this book. The reason I conducted the study and wrote this book was not to try to impress my pointy-headed constituents or to publish my findings in the journals of psychology. The purpose was, and continues to be, to provide moms, dads, teachers, and caregivers with a whole new dimension of insights into what motivates children to misbehave. More importantly, though—what motivates them to behave and how to equip parents with this knowledge. The feedback I've received from the parents who participated in the study has been that we accomplished our goals.

Whether you have a Bear, Monkey, Porcupine, Lamb, or Zebra in your habitat, your goal cannot change—do your best and trust God for the rest. I like to remind parents how simple life would have been if our kids had come into the world with a manual under one arm entitled *Instructions for the Care and Feeding of DQ Factor #____*. Even the cheapest import comes from the factory with a really nice owner's manual. We didn't even get an application for the zookeeper job.

Whenever you are feeling shaky about your zookeeping skills, keep in mind that our kids are unbelievably resilient. They are uniquely capable of maneuvering through even the craziest of childhoods (see mine) and still turn out great. You are going to make mistakes. We all do. So when you make a mistake, admit it, own it, apologize for it—and get on with it. Don't beat yourself up over your mistakes or turn in your zookeeper union card over them.

The fact that you are reading this book over sports pages, cookbooks, or cereal boxes tells me that you love your children enough to try new techniques. So take a moment, relax, and pat yourself on the back. The world is full of parents who don't care, don't realize they need help, or simply don't want to put the effort into it. Actually, when it comes right down to it, I THINK YOU ARE REMARKABLE! I hope that felt good.

Finally, take it from a zookeeper whose two animals are getting close to leaving the habitat. Whether they're sleeping like angels or causing you to pull your hair out—enjoy every precious minute with them. They are truly God's gifts.

INTERESTED IN APPEARING
IN OUR DQ VIDEO SPECIAL?

Please tell us your story. We are in the process of putting together a

DQ Factor video program that will be available commercially and provided to

schools, churches, and service organizations. If this book has helped you as a

parent, please go to *www.dreamfocus.org* and tell us your story. All submitters will

receive a free gift, plus parents whose testimonies are used in the program will

also receive a complete video series and be invited to appear in the

filming of the special. Questions, comments, or product inquiries can be

directed to Dr. Cynaumon at the above web site.

BOOKS, SPEAKING ENGAGEMENTS, AND RESOURCES

Dr. Cynaumon is available for speaking engagements

and seminars as well as TV, radio, and other interviews.

OTHER BOOKS AND PRODUCTS
BY DR. GREG CYNAUMON

God Still Speaks Through Dreams—
Are You Missing His Message?

(Thomas Nelson)

The Barnes and Noble Bible Trivia Quiz Book

(Barnes and Noble)

Empowering Single Parents

(Moody)

How to Avoid Alienating Your Kids in 10 Easy Steps

(Moody)

The Hassle Free Homework System

(The Phonics Game)

Left Behind—The Board Game Adventure

(Talicor Games)

The Dr. Laura Game

(Hasbro)